RECREATION BUSINESS

STRATEGIES FOR SUCCESS

John R. Kelly

SAGAMORE VENTURE

Publishers: Joseph J. Bannon/Peter Bannon
Sales and Marketing Manager: Misti Gilles
Marketing Assistant: Kimberly Vecchio
Director of Development and Production: Susan M. Davis
Graphic Designer: Marissa Willison
Production Coordinator: Amy S. Dagit
Technology Manager: Mark Atkinson

Library of Congress Control Number: 2018936938
ISBN print edition: 978-1-57167-919-2
ISBN ebook: 978-1-57167-918-5
Printed in the United States.

SAGAMORE ◆◆◆ VENTURE

1807 N. Federal Dr.
Urbana, IL 61801
www.sagamorepublishing.com

To all who continue to believe
there is more to life than money

Contents

PREFACE

This book is a conversation about leisure-based businesses. Several texts follow the sequential functions of forming and operating such a business. The first was my book *Recreation Business* (New York: Wiley, 1985). These books take the process step-by-step from concept through business plans, formation, financing, accounting, human resources, and evaluation. For those without business school preparation, they can be useful, if inadequate. They begin and end largely with a business point of view. Such books have a number of limitations. First, they are selective. Out of the panoply of recreation businesses, they select a few that are most common or most familiar to the authors. Second, they are out of date by the time they are in print because the field changes so rapidly. Third, they tend to be based on the "conventional wisdom" about business, usually small and retail. But recreation business is different in ways that will be made clear over and over in this volume.

This book is different. It begins with an introduction to the scope and variety of recreation businesses. Then some of the major issues about the field in general are opened for thought and discussion. The remainder of the book is based on the social and behavioral science research about recreation and leisure that has been developed since 1970. The continuing question is, how does this research guide and direct the beginning and operation of a recreation business? The unfolding of the conversation starts with how recreation is different from other goods and services, and it continues with a number of themes directed toward the formation and operation of such an enterprise. This book is directed toward the entrepreneur and those who are involved in developing recreation business strategies.

There is another critical difference. Gradually invading conventional business-school thinking is the field of behavioral economics. Counter to the traditional assumption of rational decision making in choices such as purchasing and investing, an enormous amount of research has demonstrated that many, perhaps most, such decisions are not analytical. Rather, they involve leaps to action from sets of unacknowledged assumptions, associations, and biases. Fortunately, in 2011 Daniel Kahneman, who won a Nobel Prize in economics for his pioneering work, published a very readable entry into behavioral economics. This approach informs the analysis of many of the issues of leisure entrepreneurship addressed here. (See *Thinking, Fast and Slow*, New York, NY: Farrar, Straus, and Giroux, 2011.)

One limitation to this book is that market-sector recreation is connected with two other major business sectors: travel and hospitality. Each has developed into a field with its own approaches, vocabularies, and assumptions. To include them in this volume would make it too expansive and diverse. Some recreation elements of both are legitimately included. People travel to recreation sites with recreation motivations. Hotels often provide recreation amenities and even charge for them separately from room tariffs. Resorts are, for the most part, recreation providers combined with hotels and restaurants. The recreation opportunities draw their clientele. The "wisdom" of this book is certainly applicable to such programs. However, this is not a book about travel and hospitality.

Further, it does not include everything you need to know about this limited subject. For accounting, there are professionals to hire and several computer programs oriented to smaller businesses for the electronically adept. They are available online or through business supply outlets. Nor is this a primer on all business functions. The focus on what is special about leisure and recreation omits considerable contextual information. Some readers will take business courses; others learn from experience, hopefully not the hard way. However, this book is different, as is the field of recreation business!

To a degree, what follows is one side of an imagined conversation with a senior scholar who has studied leisure and its social contexts for 5 decades. Incorporating work in sociology, social psychology, economics, and even a bit of politics, he leads the reader through a sequence of common and uncommon issues related to leisure business. As outlined in the About the Author page, his dozen books, 100-plus articles and chapters, and research and consulting are one basis for the analysis. However, almost as important, he has been observing and thinking critically outside the traditional business box for long enough to turn some traditional ideas upside down.

One other introductory item: I firmly believe that we learn best by experience and by dialogue, even debate, rather than by absorbing a book full of facts. The chapters will include some cases, usually in the form of debates and debatable issues. This book includes a number of exercises in which students will be pointed outward to examine current business practices, succeeding and failing, and the seemingly infinite variety of sources and resources on the ever present ether, still sometimes referred to as the World Wide Web. Also, the format is an attempt to facilitate the book's use in online courses. For students who are not in a group setting, the research exercises and debates can be adapted to individual responses and forays into available fields and sources of information.

The beginning is that "leisure is different." The focus is on what a recreation business sells or rents: an experience. The crucial element is quality. And decades of study have yielded a lot of insight into how leisure experiences can be raised to a level that will attract and retain clients.

John R. (Jack) Kelly
2018

CHAPTER 1:
RECREATION BUSINESS IS REALLY BIG!

Leisure is sometimes defined as free time—time left over from all the obligations of life. The problem is that there may not be any. People always have something more to do related to work, maintenance, or social responsibilities. For the most part, people choose leisure and recreation activities because they consider them worth the time and energy. Recreation business (RB) has an added dimension: a cost in money. So the constant theme for any analysis of RB is, what makes it worth the investment of time, money, energy, and forgoing other activity?

It would be convenient to be able to give a neat list of those activities for which a measurable number of people, also called a market, demonstrate a willingness to invest. One problem is that such lists seem unending. Another is that such lists change over time. For example, here is one such general list:

From community studies:

1. Six of the usual top 10 favorite activities involve some interaction with family, friends, or other regular companions:
   * Affection, intimacy, and sexual activity
   * Informal conversation
   * Informal activity with others such as walking, shopping, and eating
   * Social outings and events
   * Visiting family and friends
   * Playing with children

2. Other informal activity such as reading for pleasure; watching television or other entertainment media; partaking in electronic games and entertainments; playing outdoor sports, appropriate to age and environment; and eating out.

3. A variety of activities including religious worship and meditation, short auto trips, gardening and yard care, home decorating, shop projects, arts and crafts, hunting, fishing, entertaining at home, walking or jogging for exercise, child-centered events,

hobbies too varied to list, and (surprise) conversation and social interaction in the workplace.

Note that only a few involve business provisions. Any narrow focus on recreation businesses gives a wildly false impression: that competition for the most scarce resource, time, is only with competing businesses. Not so. More on this in Chapter 4. However, in this introduction, note that ordinary people can choose almost anything primarily because they enjoy the experience. Adding a price makes the choice all the more serious. The experience has to be "worth it."

Variety Is the Norm, Not the Exception

Another approach suggests that the wide variety of leisure requires a kind of balance. Some activities require a high-intensity effort and focus. As such, they may be central to a person's self-definition. For example, a person may be deeply involved in a sport as player or coach, in an art or craft as a creator or organizer, or in specialized travel. At the other extreme, some activities require low intensity effort and tend to be oriented toward relaxation or a change from high demand. In their overall balance, most people have both intense and relaxing engagements.

Questions

Which kind of activity is most important to you? Which kind provides the best business markets? Why?

The ordinariness of most nonwork activity does not mean that many people would not like to be more seriously engaged in outdoor sports, creative focus, challenging involvement, or even exotic environments. However, most choices are made from relatively accessible possibilities. Anything that requires financial cost, time scheduling, or forgoing other activities has to be highly valued. The implications for businesses are clear—the offered experience has to be worth it.

Scholars can debate definitions of leisure, recreation, free time, and other terms. The focus here will be on what people do, why they do it, and how businesses can contribute to the meaning and joy of people's lives through their offerings. That does not mean that there are no technical questions and issues. For example, what kinds of activities and opportunities vary significantly by age, gender, ethnicity, income, residential region, family status, education, and sexual orientation? What kinds of activities decrease with age? When is physical or mental ability a factor?

Questions

For students in residential colleges and universities, their recreation participation tends to change greatly on leaving school? How and why? Does this create or limit business opportunities?

If you are uncomfortable without definitions, here are a few to begin: Leisure is activity chosen in relative freedom for its qualities of satisfaction, that is, for the experience. Recreation is purposeful leisure activity. Recreation businesses provide goods or services in the market sector, requiring a financial return on investment.

The Scope of Leisure and Recreation

Those who have not had an introduction to the variety and range of activities and contexts of recreation and leisure may want to at least leaf through one of the introductory texts that give more depth and breadth than will be offered here. (My bias is toward one of the later editions of *Leisure* [Kelly, 2012]. The fourth edition is available from Sagamore–Venture Publishing and earlier ones from your friendly online used seller.) However, the following list may serve to suggest something of the scope of what organized engagements with business dimensions that people do:

- Shopping facilities
  - * Conventional stores
  - * Other retailers: online, catalog, outdoor markets, etc.
- Food and drink services
  - * Retail stores: specialty, party, catering
  - * Fast-food establishments: with play areas, fun themes
  - * Cafés and coffeehouses: with WiFi, meeting areas
  - * Restaurants: themes, ethnic, meeting rooms
  - * Bars and nightclubs: sports bars, student meeting places, entertainment
  - * Refreshment services at special sites and events
- Participation locales and facilities
  - * Dancing: discos, age-focused, learning styles
  - * Sports: open, membership clubs, community centers
  - * Special environments: golf and tennis clubs, fitness centers
  - * Age-focused sports
    - - Special facilities and instruction
    - - For-profit leagues and training

- Amusement parks
  * Traditional: rides, events, shows, retail food and souvenirs
  * Theme: water, wildlife exhibitions, special environments
- Museums, gardens, and parks
  * Public and private
  * Specialty and multipurpose
- Shows, towers, and tours
  * Local and regional cultural and natural sites
  * Community-based: amateur, school, themes
  * Historical sites and tours: author and celebrity tours and exhibitions
  * Traveling shows, concerts, performances
- Stadiums and racetracks
  * Dedicated: single sport or activity
  * Spectator and participant, including betting
- Hotels, resorts, and camps
  * Campgrounds and marinas
  * Hotels with recreation sites, facilities, access, programs
  * Self-contained resorts: seasonal, water-based, ski, sport, cultural
  * Spas: health and beauty enhancement
  * Travel: cruise, tours, clubs, age- or activity-focused
- Events: cultural, competitive, and environmental
- Native historical or cultural enterprises
  * Natural sites: interpretive, hiking, riding
  * Programs, shows, exhibitions, art and craft sales
- Activity and locale access
  * Flying, gliding, riding, climbing, jumping
  * Interpretive tours: bus, guiding, organizing
  * Competitions: team sports, running
- Farms, estates, and natural sites
  * Tours, visits, historical sites
  * Activity-based: guest ranches, rafting, boating
- Camps, schools, and expeditions
  * Age-graded: educational camps, adventure trips, rafting, exploring, cultural
  * Sports and arts camps

- Products and services
  * Professional services: trainers and tutors
  * Recreation products: equipment, repairs, uniforms
  * Training: online, videos, books, group and individual
  * Rentals: sites, equipment
- Media: TV, online, journals, news

Enough already! And this is not all. Any list is incomplete or inexact. The point is that we tend to focus on our own experiences and observations. Most of us have never been to Aspen or Jackson Hole for either music or skiing. Few of us have visited the great museums of Europe, either on our own or in a tour. There seem to be more and more "foodies" whose favorite recreation is eating and cooking, but most have never attended chef school or an ethnic-cuisine resort or camp. The scope and variety of business-based recreation activities seem almost infinite, not to mention the differing styles, skill levels, and locales for each activity.

> ### Challenge
>
> Name 3 or 4 more not on the list above. It's not that hard. Are there any such engagements or experiences that turn you on? It is not too early to begin thinking about this. Do you have any distant dreams, a maybe-one-day hope?

Recreation Services

That very long list is not exhaustive, but perhaps exhausting. Yet there is another entire set of recreation businesses. They are the indirect providers, the services that support and enhance the more direct providers. They are not the focus of this book, but consider them carefully. One or more may combine interests and talents more than the direct providers introduced above. Here is a partial and suggestive list:

- Market research
- Advertising
- Media: writing, reporting, producing
- Realty: developing, marketing, planning recreation-based homes and communities
- Financial services: loans, leasing, packaging
- Recreation-based vacation and second-home developments and communities
- Simple locality-based retailing: liquor, specialty foods

- Rentals: everything related to the activity, locale, and experience
- Child-care for the away-from-home recreating group or family
- Specialized skill acquisition or conditioning
- Publication: recreation-based videos, books, magazines, online experience
- Education: teaching can be satisfying, too

Research

Time to get out there in a discovery mode. Find and interview someone in an RB, preferably someone who is excited about it.

Talk with the CEO of an RB. What were their original hopes? Was there a clear plan, and has it worked out? Has financing been a problem? Personnel? Long hours? What about the future: expansion, retrenchment, more of the same? Then, how would you evaluate the past, present, and future of the business?

CHAPTER 2:
VARIETY IS OPPORTUNITY

The variety of activities, environments, cost levels, markets, and skill levels clearly makes it impossible for any one book, probably all conceivable books, to present how to begin, finance, market, operate, staff, and manage recreation businesses in general. Any claims to the contrary are either ignorant or deceptive. That is a major limitation.

On the other hand, the same variety is also opportunity! With the many different recreation businesses, there ought to be opportunity for anyone with desire and a willingness to learn and work. Further, the possibility of a return on investment is real, simply because a great deal of money is spent on leisure and recreation. **The best way for you to see some of the numbers is to go online and check out some of the totals and trends.** Search categories such as recreation expenditures, outdoor recreation trends, sports participation, and sport expenditures. The following is a sample of such current numbers, but they are only a sample. First, however, a few warnings:

- Trade organizations that depend on their industry for income frequently tend to exaggerate or at least select favorable totals and trends.
- Unfortunately, the federal government has reduced support of data for sources such as the *Statistical Abstract of the United States*, but there are still some useful online data under this rubric.
- Again, many of the best sources of trend data are proprietary and done by major market research organizations for corporations and trade associations. If you have an industry contact, try to get access. Failing that, occasional news reports reveal some such studies.
- Be careful with news reports, especially those that proclaim the "latest exploding activity," that "everyone is doing it," or any other such claim. That may make for journalism "buzz" but poor investment advice.

However, many people are spending a lot of time and money on recreation in more ways than can be easily listed. Depending on what is included, leisure and recreation is the second or third biggest sector of developed economies. Direct recreation expenditures in the United States are estimated to have grown from about $18 billion in 1960, to $41 billion in 1970, to $105 billion in 1980, to something over $200 billion currently.[1]

Further, this growth provided, according to the U.S. Bureau of Labor Statistics (n.d.), at least 15,620,000 leisure and hospitality jobs in 2016. That is about the same as in all retailing and over 3 million more than in manufacturing. The economic shift away from manufacturing employment and toward services, health, and leisure suggests that a higher percentage of jobs will be in some kind of recreation or leisure. As suggested, while millions of those jobs will be in direct service, millions more will be in support and ancillary services required by any business. Add to that uncounted elements such as the design and construction of home recreation spaces for entertainment, media, and arts. Seldom included are businesses supporting devotion to collecting and rebuilding classic cars, equipment repair for everything from cameras to dune buggies, and media-provided information on the toys, locales, organizations, and skill acquisition of all those activities and avocations.

Trends: Essential and Dangerous

Too many years ago, Kelly and Warnick (1999) did their best to analyze participation trends in about 100 common recreation activities. The analysis was based on a series of yearly surveys of over 15,000 households. The proprietary data were made available (delayed a year) for analysis. If available in a library or used, the book may still be of interest as an illustration of what might be done with such data. The trends and predictions, although mostly right, are now outdated and incomplete. Nonetheless, such national surveys yield a very general map of what has been going on. As general context, useful. As a specific guide, not so much.

---

[1]These and other statistics in this book are illustrative, not complete or final. The author has included material from multiple sources. Further, all large numbers are estimates from surveys with varying samples. The student is urged to use online searches to update, augment, and correct statistics in this text.

Research

Using the kinds of sources illustrated, try to find data on your activity of interest. Combine the results and make a prediction based on your best estimate. How confident would you be of the results? Enough to bet your money? Your life?

To assist in the process, here are a few examples of such numbers: (Unfortunately, federal support of the regular gathering and reporting of recreation statistics has been withdrawn. Table 2.1 has been adapted from the Statistical Abstracts of the United States. The data is based on a Mediamark national household market study for 2010.) Totals are in thousands (i.e., add ,000 to each total).

Table 2.1
Adult Participation in Selected Leisure Activities by Frequency: 2010

Activity	Total Number in thousands	%	At least 1/week %	At least 1/month %
Attend auto shows	19,346	8.5	0.3	0.5
Attend horse races	6,654	2.9	0.1	0.2
Billiards/pool	19,468	8.5	1.0	1.8
Bird watching	13,793	6.1	3.2	0.9
Cooking for fun	50,243	22.0	11.7	4.9
Dining out	112,477	49.3	19.0	17.6
Fantasy sports league	8,969	3.9	2.0	0.3
Go to beach	58,670	25.7	2.4	4.5
PC/computer games online with software	16,563	7.3	4.8	1.0
PC/computer games offline with software	18,971	8.3	4.8	1.5
Play cards	46,190	20.3	4.9	6.1
Reading books	86,540	37.9	24.2	6.1

There may be ongoing changes and shifts for each activity, but the overall picture changes slowly. The old social science rule is that the best predictor of future behavior is past behavior. (If you want to test this, analyze why in general the best predictor of college grades is high school grades.) Of course, national figures may not represent local participation at all. Further, for some businesses a small national percentage can obscure an adequate base for a particular activity in a given locale. On the other hand, the national data give a warning that may temper the enthusiasm of a participant who dreams that "everyone" will want to do whatever it is that he or she especially enjoys.

Outdoor recreation in federal parks, forests, seashores, and other venues is a somewhat different case. Once federal agencies other than the National Park Service realized that outdoor recreation was a major part of their mission, they began to collect entrance and user statistics. In cases such as the Corps of Engineers and the Bureau of Land Management, the amount and variety of use came as something of a surprise. In any case, the good news is that their websites offer useful comparative data on recreation usage. The not-so-good news is that tight budgets have further curtailed much needed research. (Check websites such as the U.S. Forest Service for recreation trends.)

Case: Everyone Is Sure That . . . the "Golf Boom"

In 1995, golf was booming. The "golf explosion" stimulated the opening of hundreds of new courses and clubs. Private clubs combined with upscale housing lined along fairways were especially popular. Public recreation authorities in and near cities were under pressure to build more courses, as even sunup tee times required reservations far in advance. The aging of the population added to the enthusiasm, because golf is the only popular outdoor sport that can be continued into later years by many people. Also, more women were playing. In the Kelly–Warnick trends analysis of the Simmons Market Research (Kelly & Warnick, 1999, pp. 41–42), yearly data from 1975 to 1996 demonstrated slow and steady growth, perhaps not a "boom," but more reliable as a basis for investment and development.

Identification of market segments showed increases across all age segments with the largest increases among those aged 18 to 34. Further, with college graduates playing at twice the rate of those with only high school education, and with college enrollments increasing and female growth rates exceeding male growth rates, the future looked bright. However, 20 years later, we see overexpansion, private clubs opening to daily fee players, developments becoming bankrupt, and growth stalling.

How did Kelly and Warnick (1999) do on their trend analysis? They pointed to a reduced rate of growth and limiting factors such as cost, time pressures, and the inconvenience of driving time to courses in urban areas. "How far are busy adults willing to drive to play, especially at

---

inconvenient times?" (Kelly & Warnick, 1999, pp. 41–42). We can generously give the forecasters a C- on overall prediction and perhaps an A- on identifying the factors that, along with a recession, combined to halt the boom.

Debate

In some way viable for class size or online dispersion, set up one or more debates on a popular recreation activity, preferably one that receives media attention. Have one team predict growth and give reasons for growth using as much data as possible. Have a negative team attack the proposition with questions and facts. Limit presentation time or space strictly. Nonparticipants can vote at the end. (The point is that RB investment will call for this kind of debate, even if it is internal for the investor. Also, see later explication of the premortem.)

A Walk on the Bright Side

On a more pleasant note, back to the chapter theme. There are literally hundreds of activities that people do as recreation. Most, if not all, offer some opportunity for providers and supporting businesses. Long lists are boring and pages of numbers numbing. However, here are a few that give at least a suggestion of how all the variety offers business opportunities (Table 2.2). Don't miss that there are variations from year to year.

Issue

Note which activities in the following table remain quite stable and which have significant variation. Try to explain the variations. Which changes are actually trends, that is, relatively consistent gains or losses. Explain the trends.

Any surprises? How about your favorite versus some activity you think uninteresting?

Lots of people do these and countless other activities. However, if you were to try to assess markets, what is missing here?

Table 2.2

Activity Participation in U.S. from 2000 to 2015

Activity	Total participation in U.S. (in thousands, ages 7+)			
	2000	2005	2010	2015
Exercise walking	86,296	85,991	95,803	106,321
Exercise with equipment	44,820	54,248	55,286	56,275
Running, jogging	22,812	29,246	35,542	44,545
Swimming	60,758	57,972	51,943	46,278
Work out at club	24,071	34,725	34,549	36,587
Bicycle riding	43,135	43,138	39,789	36,008
Bowling	43,133	45,383	36,728	35,219
Billiards, pool	32,548	37,259	24,014	21,465
Golf	26,401	24,671	20,298	18,585
Hunting with firearms	19,249	19,428	16,273	17,656
Boating: motor/power	24,233	27,539	20,081	14,112
Soccer	12,899	14,142	13,534	12,771
Tennis	10,032	11,121	11,136	12,309
Softball	13,979	14,092	10,841	9,751
Kayaking, rafting	3,137	7,572	5,570	9,225
Tai chi/yoga	7,058	7,111	–	7,534
Skiing: alpine	7,392	6,900	7,383	6,058
Hunting with bow & arrow	4,691	6,623	5,157	5,656
Paintball games	5,349	8,022	6,100	5,094
In-line roller skating	21,817	13,115	7,448	4,895
Martial arts	5,438	5,987	6,112	4,276
Racquetball	3,222	–	–	–
Water skiing	5,921	6,725	5,220	3,487
Ice hockey	1,939	2,432	3,299	3,739
Skiing: cross-country	2,338	1,873	2,026	2,428

Note. Data from multiple sources including Statistical Abstracts of the United States, GfK Mediamark Research (http://mri.gfk.com/), and *Outdoor Recreation Outlook 2016* by the American Recreation Coalition. (Use search engines for current sources.)

Unfortunately, we have to join the debate a little at this point. Just gross numbers may give some idea of the relative size of markets and some trends. However, there is too much missing:

- How can you identify markets by age, gender, geographical region, season, education, and income level? What other subcategories would you want to know?
- If an activity is usually done in groups, who are the usual companions?
- How much are participants willing to spend?
- What about regularity and commitment?

Of the totals in Table 2.1, how many people report participating regularly (Table 2.2)?

Table 2.2

Regular Participation in 2009

Activity	2009 in thousands
Exercise walking (110+ days/year)	30,860 of total 93,359
Work out in a club (110 days)	13,243 of total 38,020
Running/jogging (110+ days)	7,949 of total 32,212
Bicycle riding (110+ days)	4,321 of total 38,139
Tennis (30+ days)	1,665 of total 12,250
Soccer (40+ days)	5,080 of total 13,534
Hunting with firearms	5,762 of total 16,273
Golf (40+ days)	4,848 of total 21,872
Swimming (110+ days)	2,902 of total 51,943

Note. Estimates from GfK Mediamark Research, New York, NY (internet reports released 9/20/2011).

More on this in Chapter 7. However, the general observation holds for most activities. The percentage of those who do an activity regularly is roughly one fourth to one third of the total who claim to have participated at all in the past year. This suggests that gross totals of runners, tennis players, or anyone else, especially if offered by those with an interest in promoting the activity, need to be viewed in this perspective. There are a few exceptions such as dedicated distance runners, but it remains true that most recreation participants participate casually.

In the state park of Jekyll Island, Georgia, simple observation demonstrated that more and more bicyclists were coming with bikes on their car racks. Some were "spandex" riders with their many-speed bikes, colorful outfits, and determined pedaling down the roads. But there was more growth in casual or "family" cyclists, often on rental bikes and mostly on the bike paths and trails. The "Authority" responded with a development of off-road paths, and still more people came. The single rental shop was overwhelmed. Hotels added their own rentals. However, mechanical and tire repairs were lined up. In this case, a natural environment, access, alert management, and a growing activity combined into opportunity. And the market sector lagged behind, especially the casual rider market.

Is the consistent fact that for some activities only 25% of people actually do the activity on a regular basis a problem or an opportunity? How can you turn a problem into an opportunity? Use an actual RB as your case if possible.

A number of ways of dealing with the opportunities and issues suggested by these numbers will be offered beginning in Chapter 4. The summary of this chapter is relatively simple: In the U.S. alone, millions of people are doing hundreds of different activities as recreation and leisure. Behind only housing as a business, leisure and recreation vies with health, food, transportation, entertainment, and other services as the largest economic sector. (Note that several of these overlap.) Every indication is that it will grow in size and importance. As will be demonstrated later, businesses range from giant international corporations to single-person shops and services. Additionally, most people will continue to seek pleasure in their nonwork time, sometimes in self-generated activity, sometimes in groups, and sometimes supported by one or more businesses.

A Summary of the Scope of Recreation Business

The products are everywhere. In the street and on the playground, in the home and in the forest, on the water and in the air, in the sports arena and at the school, and even in the church and in the shopping center. Recreation businesses find markets in all kinds of people. Most gifts to children are related to play in some way. Older people adapt their interests and abilities to maintain interests and engagements. In between, adults with multiple responsibilities and time constraints juggle, prioritize, and eliminate to spend some time doing things they enjoy with people they value.

Here is a general list of types of recreation providers: destination attractions, travel support, residential leisure, community activity centers, outdoor sport venues, spectator sports, skill acquisition, outdoor resource sites, mechanized activities, popular culture, equipment and service retailers, food and drink locations, equipment manufacturing, and, to add a dimension, legal and illegal gambling and other shadow activities.

Expenditure estimates:
- Total in the U.S. over $200 billion/year
- Spectator sports over $12 billion/year
- Legal gambling industries $25 billion to estimates of over $40 billion/year
- Golf courses over $16 billion/year
- Skiing facilities vary around $20 billion/year
- Fitness and sports centers over $20 billion/year

Even with approximations and estimates, that's a lot of business!

CHAPTER 3:
SOME BIG ISSUES AS BACKGROUND

First, a suggestion. Some students may prefer to deal with the issues introduced in this chapter in conjunction with the final chapter on the future. "Looking Ahead" (Chapter 15) requires examination of the larger context of any business sector and of the elements of operating a recreation business (RB). Social and economic change and conflicts shape the context of any business. Distribution of income and wealth differentiate markets. Government policies involve land management, subsidies, regulations, restrictions, and education. Social changes in population affect everything. (Note the great changes in ethnic composition and location.) The gender revolution is real, if incomplete. Cities are changing in composition and geography. (There is "gentrification" and wider dispersal from former racial "ghettos" that affect recreation markets.) Terrorist actions close tourism destinations and related businesses. Ample evidence suggests that change is always continual and sometimes cataclysmic. Some contextual issues are introduced in this chapter. Others will pop up throughout the book. Deal with some of the big ones now or later, but please don't pass them over.

Debate

Which social changes have affected leisure and recreation the most? Racial resistance? Sexual revolution? Education inclusion? Aging population? Title 9? Electronics? Globalization? Ethnic diversity? Others? All the above? Why?

What Are Markets?

Business means markets. No market, no business. This sounds simple and obvious, but it is not. Markets are individuals, groups, and organizations willing and able to pay for goods and services. Still simple? What about that phrase *willing and able*? *Willing* means having interest, knowledge, social support, and motivation. That is, it is a matter of culture as well as choice. *Able* means having disposable income, but also physical and mental ability and either skill or access to learning. The individual may make the buying decision, but do so in social, cultural, and economic contexts.

Now, not so simple. For example, some years ago a market research organization developed a marketing prediction model that focused on residential enclaves. It was based on the simple premise that neighborhoods usually reflect more than geography. Rather, residential enclaves are defined, to begin with, by income. Further, residential areas often have a general lifestyle. That style comprises family, especially age or absence of children; education including quality and prestige as well as level; cultural factors such as ethnicity and religion; and, surprisingly to some traditionalists, leisure investments and styles. Leisure, in this model, serves as a social identity symbol and context for a range of other more traditional market indices. The point is that recreation is not some separate set of choices and engagements. Rather, it is enmeshed in an interlocked set of preferences (culture), resources (the economy), and opportunities and experiences (social). For our purpose, the context of leisure markets is cultural, social, political, and economic.

Issue

Where did you begin and learn your favorite recreation activities?
- School? Quality and style are largely determined by residential income levels.
- Family? Part of a cultural history.
- By paying for an opportunity or access to a site? Economic factors such as income level and household requirements.

Issues of the Larger Context

In general, the relationship of recreation to the public sector (i.e., the many levels of government) is obvious:
- The introduction and beginning skills of so many sports, arts, and interests are in school.
- The community provides many of the dedicated spaces for sports, meeting places, and other activities. This is partly a matter of social equity and partly economic efficiency. Fields, gyms, and other facilities get the most use at the lowest cost when they are designated as public.
- Natural environments such as national and state parks are best protected and utilized by specialized agencies that can balance

conservation with use and access. A U.S. Forest Service slogan was "land of many uses."

- Health and safety regulations and emergency provisions protect all users, not just those who can afford special services.

This means that recreation has political dimensions. How much of a community, state, or federal budget is allocated for recreation opportunities? Which resources are given priority, and are priorities decided by an open political process or by insiders who "pay to play"? At what level is the planning, funding, management, and environmental support determined for, as an example, a reservoir near a city? Which recreational activities are considered too harmful or dangerous to be supported or allowed? Are any drugs legitimately recreational? Is a sport with serious long-term injury problems to be supported or permitted? If dogfights are banned and seen as cruelty to animals, what about sports that involve similar combat of people?

There is, however, a greater issue. If the estimate is accurate that 97% of recreational spending in the United States is in the market sector, is this an optimal (im)balance?

**Debate: Pro or con –
The market allocates recreation resources best.**

YES

- The market is most responsive to the wants and preferences of the consumer. The consumer enters the market able to make an immediate decision on purchase. The consumer decides on priorities. Individuals and households recognize scarcity of resources—in the case of recreation, time and money. A bureaucracy, on the other hand, is far removed from the consumer and is, at best, cumbersome. Market decisions made by the people who will use the product require no complex process, no special expertise, and no costly bureaucracy.
- The sovereign consumer is the right locus of decision. No one should decide whether others prefer hiking boots or concert tickets. In some areas (e.g., medical care), there may be need for expert knowledge. In leisure and recreation, there is none. Only the person involved can assess the value of an experience. Further, the market maximizes freedom. However benevolent, government is oriented toward control of some sort. "Experts" may make a career of asserting they

---

know more than ordinary people. If there is any area of life in which we ought to be able to make our own decisions, it is what we do for pleasure.

- The market is immediate and flexible. Bureaucracies are slow. If we want to try something new, the controlling agency may resist. The market, however, will respond most quickly. In fact, the market system is always in the process of developing new goods and services. The profit motive is a great stimulus for innovation.

- The market is relatively free from political trading. Regulations are needed for some kinds of activity. However, through the portable media of money and credit, the market works through the exchange of goods and services. In some cities, public recreation is used to buy votes rather than respond to evident need. In totalitarian countries, recreation is used to quiet dissent. Combining political and economic power can be inequitable and even dangerous. Adding privilege to political power can be inefficient and unjust.

- Even public recreation is moving more toward a fee-for-services basis of allocation. Using a quasi-market system enables public agencies to pay for programs and facilities without tax increases. Also, those who pay demonstrate their priorities. Because there are no fully accurate ways of measuring preferences and values of large populations, the market provides the most direct measure.

- Market economists have an answer to the problem of inequalities and inequities of income and wealth. They argue that the proper economic response to inequity in opportunity is not for providers to provide opportunities free or at a subsidized rate, but to address the distribution of income through taxation policies and subsidies so that everyone has the resources to act as a sovereign consumer. (Traditional economists usually dismiss the political problems with this with some form of "that's not our problem.")

- The market is the basis of the social system. Society exists through the exchange of goods and services (i.e., the market system, the division of labor, and money as a medium of exchange). The market may at times become unbalanced and overproduce or misdistribute. However, the best course of action is for the market to self-correct rather than force an adjustment. In the meantime, the market generally has enough flexibility for consumers to adjust their lives to what is available.

NO

- The market seeks a return on investment, not the development of human life. Recreation is more than consumption. It is a developmental or existential fundamental to human life (i.e., re-creation). The market responds to price, not need. Resources are allocated according to potential profit, not the potential to support and enhance life. The toy or faddish geegaw that offers a high profit margin may have little to do with the dimensions of human action, significant bonding with others, and personal development. There is little profit in open space or forest paths, but the potential for human life may be immeasurable.

- The market creates an imbalance in investment. On a different level, the market does not allocate resources for education, because children produce little direct profit. Rather, we believe that it is good for society that all children be educated, not just those whose families can pay high fees. The market does not allocate well for all elements of the common good. The same is true for recreation. Do we want only the children of the wealthy to learn to sing, dance, and play sports? Do we want only the suburbs to have open space? Do we want only a few to see the Grand Canyon? If it were up to the market, we would have more of Las Vegas and less of Yellowstone, because gambling produces a higher profit than camping. Try to imagine what our communities and country would be like if we were to evaluate every resource decision solely by the demonstrated ability of the resource to produce a high monetary return.

- The market emphasizes commodity-intensive activity. The market promotes jet skis and powerboats—not swimming. It stresses expensive electronics—not playing the guitar. The market sells uniforms and equipment—not space for children to organize their own games. Further, the "best" equipment with its logos and stripes go out of style quickly. The more expensive and temporary the equipment, the better. Yet walking is one of the few activities increasing in participation. There is no known correlation between the cost of equipment and satisfaction, short or long term.

- Further, the market responds to high-end consumers first. Those who have the money to pay high prices for equipment, locales, access, clothing, and other such items receive disproportionate attention in a market economy. Observe the investment surge toward high-end resorts tied to expensive recreation venues and facilities, rather than campgrounds near public beaches. That is why the multimillion-dollar resorts and cruises with gourmet cuisine, uncrowded space, and more serving staff than clients are proliferating. Opportunities for the wealthy are overbuilt, whereas the middle mass experiences crowding. In time, the market expands to lower income consumers, but without the privacy and pampering. Priority, however, always goes to those who can pay the most and to yielding the highest return on investment. (For example, as a pilot, I spend some time around airports and pilot lounges where I often find private and corporate jet pilots waiting, sometime for hours, for their wealthy clients. Contrast this with the crowding, delays, lines, and minimal services of commercial airline travel. Also, check the prices of private and business in online broker sites. Try "Gulfstream sales.")

- The market is short term. Corporations seek profits this quarter and this year—not a decade down the line. As a consequence, resources tend to be overused and even badly degraded for the market to maximize current use and income. When a resource (e.g., national parks) is to be preserved for generations to come, the market does not tend to manage well. Further, the market often uses land and other resources intensively rather than for sustainability. Planning and management for the long term is imperfect at best, but seldom done well by those with corporate investors given first priority. Planning takes the long view when done well; the market usually takes the short view. It is, by definition, immediate.

- The market is inequitable. Few would defend a system in which stock sales produce higher incomes than teaching or dealing 21 more than caring for the old and infirm. Also, a market distribution is dependent on available income and credit. Those with chronic health conditions have little credit left for recreation. Even caregivers need a break. The market makes no allowances for anything, especially not for need. In the United States with its enormous and increasing differences in income, the gap between the wealthy (upper 20%, 5%, 1%, or .1%,) and the lower 20% or 80% is widening. Fully 20% of households are poor, lacking even resources for adequate housing or nutrition. (Check the U.S. Census Bureau website for more statistics.) To distribute all of any good entirely by market price is inevitably inequitable. Until the income distribution is changed, the market at least has to be augmented by tax-subsidized goods and services.

Take your time with this debate. It raises a number of issues that are significant for understanding the economic context of RB. Which arguments are decisive for you, or is it really not an either-or question?

! A Question From a Different Perspective

In what ways are public and market providers complementary rather than competing? In communities? In preservation and management of land and water resources for recreation? How is an us-versus-them perspective harmful?

Other "Macro" Issues

Perspective is everything. Any problem or question can be approached in multiple ways. Even "just the facts" has multiple meanings and outcomes. What follows is not an attempt to close off perspectives, but to offer alternative perspectives on leisure, recreation, and business.

Some market sector enterprises require little capital when they consist primarily of services, use rented facilities, and require the investment of long hours. Most, however, require some investment capital. In general, such investment should yield a return at least as high as an interest-bearing account or mutual fund. Further, because the risk in such investments is low, an added return for the risk in a business investment is needed. For example, assuming that the failure rate of a firm supplying recreation equipment is 40%, a profit rate of 15% would seem reasonable to compensate for the risk.

There are other factors in investment. Business owner-operators should calculate their own income at a reasonable salary assuming that other employment is foregone. Also, a business should make provision for the generation of future capital for expansion or depreciation of stock and equipment. As a result, factors of interest—for payment of a loan or other investment return—require a consistent margin of profit if the business is to continue. More later on the calculated planning needed.

For these and other reasons, capital tends to flow toward the greatest possibilities of return on investment. That is fundamental to capitalism. In RB planning, at times an individual may choose to invest in a particular business because of the lifestyle it engenders or the environment of its location. Living near a ski slope or in a special urban neighborhood may be more important than rate of return. However, no business can withstand continual losses.

Further, many recreation businesses have peculiarities. Some are seasonal and require a high rate of profit to compensate for months of little or no income. This is why ski resort areas in Colorado try to develop summer activities. Some businesses are capital intensive and require heavy front-end investment in land, facilities, or equipment. Such enterprises usually have significant loans to pay off each month. Other businesses are labor intensive with all the financial requirements of such employment.

The issue is this: Which opportunities are most likely to attract investment capital? The answer is largely financial. For banks and other lenders, return attracts investment. This is why: Until some recent failures, eagerness to invest in gambling enterprises has been high. The profit margin and success rate have been uniquely high. (Failures such as Atlantic City illustrate, on the other hand, that location, competition, quality, and overexpansion are relevant, even in gambling.) Most business developers, especially if attempting to attract investment, have to consider long-term profits and ongoing cash flow.

Some investments promise a quick return. These businesses are responsive to a large and proven market in an area with minimal competition. Such enterprises ought to yield a rapid amortization of investment with tax advantages and thus recover capital costs and grow profit margins. Other enterprises may combine immediate markets with long-term appreciation of resources. For example, golf course developments, seashore motels, and waterfront boat facilities tend to gain in value while their income provides ongoing profit.

To this, one may respond, "So what?" That is the nature of business. There are at least several concerns for the investor. First, businesses tend to locate in markets of higher income, leaving lower income households without opportunities. Second, activities that may produce the greatest personal development, especially for children and adolescents, are unfunded—profit becomes the sole criterion for investment. Third, some activities with the highest return may have harmful consequences. (There may be huge profits in drug distribution, sex tourism, gambling, blood sports, and walled resorts closing resources to local residents, to name a few.) Fourth, capital flows to large markets and high fees rather than to niche markets and recreation specialties based on skill development and personal growth.

The Investment Imbalance

In some of his earlier writing, John Kenneth Galbraith (1958) analyzed one of the limitations of capitalism. He called it the investment imbalance. If the estimate that 97% of recreation expenditures are in the market sector and that the federal government allocates roughly .003% of expenditures directly on recreation, then the issue seems obvious.

Business, not public policy, is the focus of this book. However, the imbalance has implications for business and for society. Here a few of the concerns:

- Use of fragile natural resources for short-term projects may damage them irreparably for eventual recreation use and enjoyment.
- Underfunding of recreation programs and resources in low-income areas will, in the long run, reduce the markets for many developmental and expressive activities. Perhaps the developmental values associated with some sports, arts, natural environments, and extraordinary experiences are limited to those in households with adequate discretionary income.
- The overall investment for recreation and leisure is skewed toward the highest incomes and wealth. Scarce natural resources such as beaches, forests, mountaintops, concerts, and exhibitions are out-of-bounds for even mid-income households. More capital is invested in businesses that are exclusive, extremely high cost, and even closed to nonmembers.

- Private ownership rather than public stewardship forecloses use of prime opportunities to those who cannot pay high fees. Even local residents no longer have access to opportunities that had long been open to all.

If we begin with the premise that like education, health care, housing, and nutrition, recreation is fundamental to human life, then inadequate investment in the public sector is a real and serious problem for society. Lives deprived at any stage are less productive, healthy, and satisfied than those able to choose among opportunities. Remember that phrase "Life, Liberty and the pursuit of Happiness"? Historians inform us that the happiness bit was contentious even at the founding of the United States. It still is. If we believe that active, involving, expressive, and developing physical and mental activity are really essential, then there is a public interest and responsibility. Not just for children, but through the life course and into later years, leisure and recreation opportunity is a public interest. If there is an investment imbalance, then it concerns the entire society.

Research

Investigate the percentage of your city's or town's budget that is directed to recreation. Does this reflect your values?

Go online to locate two or three major corporate recreation providers. Check the prices of deluxe cruises marketed by the not-for-profit National Geographic Society. Look for costs of special camps and expeditions that involve development and adventure for children and adolescents. Should such experiences be limited by discretionary income?

Compare the National Park Service budget for anything more than maintenance with costs of major upscale resorts and high-service hotels.

Can you think of any low-cost recreation activities that offer a profitable business opportunity because of the large potential markets?

Again, in the market sector, money flows toward the highest return. The question is, should that be the sole criterion for recreation-based investment? Does maximum investment always produce the maximum personal investment? If not, what kinds of public policies may help redress the imbalance? In the long run, inadequate public investment will lead to limited markets for many kinds of recreation.

Leisure Resources and Long-Range Planning

When an investment is made in any business, a schedule is projected for a recovery of the investment. Because some of the capital is usually borrowed, the lending institution is usually involved in developing that schedule. In some cases, large corporations have a line of credit with a bank or financial house. This line of credit enables them to meet ongoing expenses of establishing a new enterprise, without having to utilize their own resources. Such borrowing requires that the new businesses return enough income to meet the repayment schedule.

As a consequence, the RB will attempt to maximize the use of its site and service to gain as wide a clientele as possible as quickly as possible. Advertising, websites, promotions, group discounts, tour packages, price leaders, and all the other strategies will be employed to get the enterprise under way. Prices are set in a scheme that will attract clients with price and with the recreation experience.

In some cases, such pressure can lessen or eliminate concern with the central resource on which the business is based. This is especially likely when the activities are dependent on a natural environment that is fragile. The attractiveness may be eroded by crowding. Water quality is especially subject to degradation by overuse. Many examples of once attractive environments such as the south coast of Spain have given away their allure to maximize business revenues. Yosemite is only one special place where some form of visitor rationing is necessary to preserve or recover the experience and the resource itself. Sometimes, recovery itself is no longer possible.

> ## Issue
>
> What might be the result if a major attraction such as Yellowstone or the Grand Canyon were turned over to a corporation such as Disney or Six Flags?

Long-term considerations may require restricted use or limited development of a resource. More is not always better, even more visitors and clients. The nature of shareholder capitalism is to judge management a quarter or a year at a time. A business will usually have a plan for the future, but investors seldom look that far ahead. Or projected growth, urban or rural, may call for setting aside land or another resource to preserve it for use a decade or more in the future. Once land is committed, it may be lost for other uses. A growing city may need outlying land for future parks. A state may close a marshland to future development to preserve the overall ecology of a bay and its tributaries. The federal agency may close an area to camping so a fragile watershed will not be damaged.

Unless public agencies undertake this kind of planning for the future and the common welfare, the resource base for public and business recreation will be cut off in coming years. Note that even nonprofit land and resource conservation trusts depend on government tax policies that encourage and enable donations of land and money. When price and market are in control of resources, the future tends to give way to meeting current obligations and maximizing current revenue.

Debate

In another approach to the market-versus-public debate, try this. If the market allocates best, why do so many businesses fail? For example, look for examples of overexpansion. A successful business may become overconfident and expand without assessing its viable market. Why do developers so often build too many hotels when one or two are successful? Why were too many golf courses built? On the other hand, is there evidence that public planners would do better? (There is a wonderful test case going on in China where whole cities and resorts are being built by government fiat. Command economies do not have perfect records either.)

Status Symbolism and Leisure Consumption

Thorstein Veblen (1899/1953), a critical sociologist of over 100 years ago, argued that status symbolism requires owning and displaying things one does not need. In particular, as houses, cars, and travel become more common, the focus turns to leisure and recreation and to "style." By their "conspicuous waste," these things provide symbols of affluence and success. The newer slogan of "he who owns the most toys wins" turns to "s/he who shows off the most toys wins, and everyone can see it." (For example, why trade in a $200 million mega-yacht to own a $300 million one?)

When Veblen wrote his book, the leisure class was restricted in size. Discretionary income of real size was possessed mostly by the financiers of the Gilded Age, the industrialists of the manufacturing revolution, and a few super-rich from railroad and mineral development. They built mansions, recreated at segregated resorts such as Newport or Jekyll

Island (or even owned their own barrier islands), were listed in the New York "500," and were often referred to as plutocrats. Today, those with that level of investment and discretionary income are limited to that .01% or 1% at the top of the income ladder. A recent analysis demonstrates that the new affluent class includes an entire range of those with skills or experience that makes them expensive to replace (technology) and canny or lucky investors or developers (Reeves, 2017).

However, the heart of Veblen's thesis still seems relevant. In a suburb where all homes look much alike, cars appear luxurious, and kids all wear jeans to the same school, status symbols are sought elsewhere. All children are not brightly successful or athletic. New symbols of success are sought. Not just any trip, but the luxury cruise or exclusive resort, a quick skiing weekend, the built-in bar and party room with a BIG screen, the useless sports car with the exotic label, the limited club membership, and, perhaps most of all, the recreation togs with the "right" label that are clearly this year's style. After all, style means purchase for show, not use.

The issue is that leisure and recreation may become primarily consumption rather than action. When recreation becomes defined and valued primarily by expenditure rather than experience, it is said to be commodified. It is measured more by possessions than by relationships, more by price than personal development. For some people with ample discretionary income, many of the expenditures that have increased are for leisure that is exclusive and demonstrably costly. Demanding pursuits remain central for relatively small devotees.

Major investments are being made in high-end provisions such as resort hotels tied to expensive golf meccas and ski developments surrounded by exclusive name-brand and designer shops. The wave of the future may be the optic onslaught of electronic entertainment for the home. Meanwhile suppliers of sports apparel and equipment put their labels on goods that claim to be new and different each market year. As a consequence of all this, a high proportion of investment is price intensive rather than experience intensive. It is directed toward activities that have direct economic costs for locales, environments, services, equipment, and the right stuff to wear.

The problem is equating recreation with purchase rather than experience. One cost of such commodification can be that the valuable resource of time, as well as money, is directed toward possession and show more than development and engagement.

So what does this have to do with RB strategies? A persistent aim of this book is to stress the development and running of recreation businesses to maximize the experience. The premise is that such a business will gain loyal clients and outlast the flashy faddists. Most of the rest of the book is directed toward business strategies that attempt to do just that.

Debate

One side might take the point of view that price and satisfaction are closely correlated, that willingness to pay is the best measure of quality. The other side would argue that consumers are led (or misled) by promotion and advertising that stress glamour, social approval, and prestige. Such an approach may bring in customers, but they do not tend to last. Each side ought to attempt to give current examples of their position's validity.

Issue

What kind of recreation resources are available to those least able to pay? What low-cost activities could offer a profit on investment because of the size of the potential market?

Another Issue

Assuming that neither the market or public planning is infallible, is there an optimal combination of the two? Any examples of this?

Case: Pick the Winner

Here are the somewhat altered stories of two ski-based recreation enterprises. Which do you think was most successful? Why? (As a class or individual, pick the winner.)

I. A Growing Base and Accessibility

Some years ago, cross-country skiing was an activity increasing in appeal and markets. Places it could be done were more widespread for Nordic than for Alpine skiing, especially in New England and the Midwest. So a recognized expert developed what was intended to be a venue of the highest quality. Within driving distance of major urban markets such as Chicago and the Twin Cities, it would combine sets of trails for every level of ability, quality lodging, excellent cuisine, an experienced staff, and a full set of special events to publicize the center. It was QUALITY all the way. Further, the facilities and program would continually grow and develop as the market grew and the center would become recognized worldwide with its international competition event.

2. One Man's Dream

A famous newscaster, born and raised in Montana, dreamed of a resort in a mountain valley near Yellowstone that would combine the natural environments of the region with an immersion in the kind of activities he loved: riding, hiking, fishing, hunting, and enjoying the natural beauty. The architectural style would remain rustic although fully equipped with comforts. There might be added Nordic and Alpine skiing and possibly golf. The great challenge was location. It was at least 1,000 miles from any urban center except Denver, which has its own mountains and resorts. The nearest airport had minimal airline service. And there were no ancillary attractions except that great park to the south.

No cheating now! Which plan would you think most likely to succeed? In which would you have invested?

You can look them up on your browser, both their websites and Wikipedia. Here are some clues:

1. Telemark never fulfilled its founder's dreams. There were some "black swans" of fires and other damaging events. The founder was a man of great dreams who continued to invest and expand beyond what was being demonstrated as a real but limited market. The activity base did not develop as hoped. For any kind of skiing, the lack of snow or too much in storms can significantly reduce a season. And, possibly, the proliferation of recreation-serving air services made flying 1,500 miles seem as easy as driving 400.

2. Big Sky is, of course, a great commercial success. Chet Huntley's early death left it in the hands of his young wife and her advisers. His dream was transformed into plans for an upscale resort that has grown and grown. Its location is western, but the winter ski and summer golf opportunities dominate. It draws condo owners and visitors from all over North America and farther who respond to its luxury and price-limited clientele. Of course, the Bozeman airline service has multiplied and the airport accommodates all those private jets.

Questions

What might have been the signs of serious problems as Telemark grew and then failed to grow further?

As a business Big Sky is a great success. What are the elements that contributed to its success? How has it overcome seasonality?

If "location, location" is so important, what factors can overcome it? How about "quality, quality"? Any examples in your experience?

CHAPTER 4:
LEISURE IS DIFFERENT!

Is leisure business (LB) a big deal? Isn't it an adjunct to the business of manufacturing and associated businesses of transportation, construction, housing, and maybe communications? Of course, there is now general recognition that services are areas of major growth: especially health care and those aimed at the growing "senior" populations. But leisure and recreation? Aren't they the leftovers after everything necessary and important is provided?

Not for those people seeking an investment opportunity . . . or even a job. If the manufacturing sector of the U.S. economy is roughly 9% of the total, that leaves 91% for all of those services. For LB, business that is based on what people choose to do for the satisfactions in the activity (Kelly, 2012), even narrow definitions yield estimates of well over $2 trillion a year in the U.S. alone. Further, leisure spending in the market sector is estimated at 97% of the total, with public sector spending the small end of the total. LB, then, is a big deal with lots of opportunities. Add the international markets and opportunities in this truly global economy and society, and the case for importance seems self-evident.

By narrow definitions, leisure includes sports, games, concerts, the arts, leisure travel, and home entertainment. What about all the space, design, and implements in the residence that are built and maintained for leisure purposes? What about the proportion of transportation expenditures, and those symbols of the playing self such as cars, other "big toys," apparel, and eating out in themed or exclusive environments? It is no longer necessary to convince car manufacturers that they are selling status symbols, lifestyle identification, and just plain fun. The clothing market sells styles symbolizing play, to be worn in other environments. Housing is chosen for access to leisure as well as good schools. Parents brag about their kids' sports and arts accomplishments and devote time and money to support the activities.

Enough already? This book is not about trivial stuff. All of these venues offer countless opportunities for financial investment and for self-investment in economic engagement that is interesting and satisfying. The scales of LB are global and local. The capital requirements are gigantic for a destination resort and tiny for an equipment repair business.

> **Question**
>
> Would a list of leisure-based businesses be possible? Would it run into the 1000s?
>
> **Hint:** Don't stop with lists of activities or environments.

How Is Leisure Different?

Recreation business (RB) is not like selling refrigerators or servicing cars. The conventional approach to this market sector is applying the usual functions of business, especially entrepreneurship, in conventional ways. Of course, there is validity in this. But it is not enough! Failure to recognize the differences is a recipe for failure. This book is different. Rather than beginning with the conventional business functions, it is based on the dimensions and meanings of leisure and recreation.

No quick course can cover in any completeness all of the elements of beginning and operating a business. In business school, at least a full term is devoted to market research and identification and then another to financing, a third to advertising, a fourth to accounting, a fifth to staffing and personnel management, a sixth to legal environments, and so on. This relatively brief introduction offers recreation-based approaches to marketing and management. Accounting is now either managed by specialists or self-taught through online programs. The complications of tax law may be introduced in such programs or referred to professionals. Business is not simple or intuitive.

However, leisure and recreation businesses are different in significant ways. Ignoring or taking them for granted is a prelude to disaster. So let's begin the exploration.

Rule 1: No One Has to Do It

This rule is so simple and self-evident that its significance is frequently overlooked. For a car seller, the product is necessary for functioning in most urban and rural locales. Getting to work, medical care, food suppliers, social events, and leisure venues usually requires a car. Everyone knows this. So marketing is competitive, not singular. Will the buyer buy this car against possibilities of other new models, less costly used ones, or fixing the old one? The seller has to take alternatives into account, but in the case of the car seller, not walking or biking for most households. The marketing context is similar for most goods such as food, housing, maintenance, and even health care. But not for leisure!

As the old saying about long life goes, consider the alternative. The alternative for leisure engagement may be a different activity or location, that is, *substitution*. The substitute for golf may be walking, a "good walk not spoiled." Pickup basketball may replace weight lifting; a picnic, not a restaurant; recordings, not a concert; a driving trip, not a tour or cruise; or a nearby state park, not a distant national forest.

There is the default alternative: watching television, which still takes over 2 hours a day for most adults. It is cheap and accessible. Now streaming multiplies the possibilities. That is not trivial when most people have limited discretionary income and other demands on their time. More on this later, but it is important for the recreation provider to consider the wide range of alternatives when planning an RB resource.

There is the ultimate alternative: not doing it or doing a substitute. After all, leisure engagement is a choice. At any given time, a person may not find enough attraction in doing something to overcome inertia. This is the fundamental theme of this book: RB has to be attractive. The basic question is, how can a business increase its drawing power? How can satisfaction be increased and dissatisfaction minimized? Remember, no one has to do it.

The old market economics formula was supply rises to meet demand. It assumes that the demand exists and business responds. For leisure, however, demand for a product may not be evident. Obviously, if it does not exist, demand is immeasurable. Again, entrepreneurs are not just trying to beat the competition for established markets with measured trends. New leisure is not necessary.

The "revised" business formula is reversed: Supply creates demand. John Kenneth Galbraith pointed this out decades ago, but some traditionalists still resist. It should be self-evident. What business can afford to invest in a new product unless it believes that with the attractiveness of what it wants to sell, a profitable market will be created? The first function of advertising is announcing a market opportunity. Supporters of advertising costs call this education. A second function is making the offering seem attractive. So a market is, or is not, created. This revision is crucial for understanding RB: The opportunity has to be attractive, not just useful and never necessary.

Select a market area. Then identify a recreation activity for which there is no resource. How would you introduce a resource to induce players to devote time and money to this new opportunity? (More on this later, but remember, no one has to do it.)

The fundamental Rule 1 is only the beginning. At least eight more rules (to keep it simple) are essential for the development of good LB investment and operation strategies. All are not exclusive to leisure, but all have some special characteristics in the leisure context. Some are primarily oriented to concept development, some to marketing, and some to management. Some apply to all three business functions.

Common to all the rules, in developing or operating an RB you ignore them at your peril. Failure rates are daunting. In business and entrepreneurship courses and texts, the primary cause of failure is usually said to be insufficient capitalization. That is, businesses run out of money. However, I would suggest that they run out of money at least partly because they do not have enough revenue. (Obvious.) They also run out of money because they do not attract and keep enough buyers for their product or service. Most basic, then, would seem to be the failure of the provider to develop and operate a business that attracts and holds a viable market. Again, ignore these planning and operating rules at your peril!

(Note that all the rules are being introduced here and will be explained and illustrated further in following chapters.)

Rule 2: The Activity Life Cycle

The concept of the product life cycle is familiar to business students. Any new product has an introduction, growth, peak, and fall back to near zero or to a plateau that yields an adequate market base. All products have limited growth due to stimulated competition, limits on use or cost, or, in some cases, their faddish nature. For investors, the trick is to know fads from viable demand. Remember, an LB is based on people "doing leisure."

All leisure activities have the same pattern. They may be new or improvements on what is already available. They are introduced, promoted, grow, peak, and fall back to some level. No activity or product continues growing without limits. All straight-line forecasts of growth are wrong. No exceptions! Anyone who promotes the newest opportunity as limitless is ignorant, is overenthusiastic, or has something to sell.

Rule 3: "Location, Location . . ."

The old real-estate rule applies to RB. As will be analyzed more further on, if you build it in the wrong place, they probably won't come. In fact, they (target markets) may not find it. This rule has several variations depending on the distribution of potential clients, access, barriers, and how the business matches its activity base. The point, however, is simple: A good concept in the wrong place is liable to fail. A corollary is that the offering in the right place still needs to look attractive, what real-estate people call curb appeal.

Rule 4: "For Everything There Is a Season . . ."

The island on which I summer has an effective summer season of about seven weeks. Efforts to develop secondary seasons have met limited response. Therefore, a primary question to put to any business proposal is, can the business make a profit in such a brief time? The seasonal limit may be caused by varying temperatures, limited winter access, extended summer heat, or access factors. It also works two ways. If the activity is outdoors, climate variations may rule. If indoors, outdoor activity competition may place limits. In any case, many (maybe most) leisure businesses have peak seasons of limited duration or at least peaks and valleys in demand.

!

Case

Your dream is to have a dive and snorkel rent, sales, and instruction business near the many wrecks in the Great Lakes. But the season is short, 3 months at the most. Investment costs are high. What is the answer? One operator solved it with a big truck and a second location in another location, the Caribbean.

Rule 5: The 80–20 Rule Revisited

Let me admit to a seeming contradiction in this book. On the one hand, the book emphasizes baseline statistics as a corrective to overly enthusiastic estimates, the hopes-and-dreams scenarios. On the other hand (note that I, too, am a "two-handed economist"), realistic markets may be hidden behind aggregate statistics. The useful Statistical Abstracts of the United States (available free online from your helpful federal government) offer estimated numbers of participants in a wide range of leisure activities, usually with trend information. However, careful analysis of household survey data (Kelly & Warnick, 1999) has demonstrated that only 20 to 25% of these participants engage in the activity with any regularity, even in season.

The 80–20 rule of marketing suggests that only 20% of most markets provide 80% of the buyers or clients. The proportion is about the same for leisure engagement and provides a necessary corrective to optimistic claims of potential markets. Of course, it is also true that the 80% may be the best target to try to increase the market size.

Rule 6: Begin With the Right Numbers

This rule is derived from the previous rules. I provide examples later, but the fundamental rule is simple: Get the best and most reliable numbers you can find. There is no substitute for good statistics on just about anything. Nor are interpretations necessarily complicated. (See discussion on Bayesian statistics in the Errors to Avoid section in Chapter 5.)

One issue is, whose statistics? It pays to be skeptical even of what appear to be good hard numbers. Those whose profits depend on selling a service, product, or investment opportunity may take decent numbers and arrange them to their advantage. The oft quoted rules of "follow the money" and "consider the source" call for asking the hardest questions of any so-called facts. Numbers do not automatically produce science.

Rule 7: Specialization or the "Half of 1% Rule"

Another partial contradiction to Rule 6 rests partly on the 80–20 rule and partly on the peculiar nature of leisure engagement. The right business in the right place may prosper based on a "minority" activity or a special environment. Activities such as rock climbing, at least until the last few years, engage less than half of 1% of the adult population. Such activities do not appear on lists or aggregate summaries. In some cases, they may be confined to special areas, and successful businesses such as windsurfing may be clustered in a place such as Hood River, Oregon. The niches may also be a sign of possible future growth, subject to limits. Niche markets are often based on relatively small numbers with high levels of commitment and personal identification such as the "specialists" and "amateurs" described in Chapter 7. The point is that numbers are important, but in their social and economic contexts.

Rule 8: Quality Is Everything!

Rule 8, of course, follows from Rule 1. No one has to do it, so second best will fail and mediocrity is a risky strategy. Sometimes price alone can capture a segment of a large market, but for start-ups and long-term growth, quality is central. If the experience is not powerful enough to bring people back and to stimulate spontaneous word-of-mouth and person-to-person promotion, the likelihood of success is small. The many elements of quality and the nature of positive experiences will be addressed in later chapters. But the central point is so basic to RB investment and management strategies that it recurs throughout the book.

Rule 9: Experience Is a Process

Many survey instruments ask questions about satisfaction. For the most part, they allow only summations: "Overall, on a 10-point scale, how satisfied were you with the (cruise, motel, salesperson, etc.)?" The problem is that consumer engagement at the fitness center, on the wilderness hike, or at the concert is a process made up of several components. Later, the importance of the final phase of a leisure event will be found to have disproportionate weight in overall satisfaction. Now, accept that any experience usually has several dimensions that rise and fall throughout the process. A few highs may outweigh even common boredom. The factors that produce highs and lows will be introduced and examined in ways that suggest what recreation providers can plan for in designing satisfying experiences.

Question

Are all the rules equally important, or do they vary in salience for different kinds of activities and settings? Without looking ahead, which grab your attention and why?

Clue: The most important elements of satisfaction may not be the same for all kinds of leisure experiences. What activities and settings do you have in mind?

Hint: You may be biased by your own history of engagement satisfaction.

Exercise: Pick an activity-based business and write a paragraph explaining how to apply two or three of the aforementioned rules.

Of course, rules are perspectives or people's way of looking at whatever they are thinking about. (The technical term is *heuristic devices*.) The following chapters are different; they do not rest on conventional business or economic assumptions, but on some psychological, sociological, anthropological, and other social and behavioral science research and approaches. Cross-disciplines such as behavioral and sociological economics emerge as basic. The rationale for this is the nature of what the business is attempting to sell: a quality experience worth paying for.

Why is this approach useful? It provides analysis grounded in human experience rather than abstracted models. Practically, it offers recreation providers one way to minimize failure and to beat the odds. It may also be the best way for recreation providers to develop the basis for experiences that attract clients and bring them back.

Let's think about all of this in greater detail.

CHAPTER 5:
THINKING ABOUT IT

Even neat rules such as those introduced in Chapter 4 may be deceptive. When we get down to cases, thinking critically and constructively may be harder than we think. This chapter gets us further into the process.

To begin, creating business success requires more than enthusiasm and hard work. By a common estimate, close to 80% of new businesses fail within 2 years. Some reports indicate that 35% are still in business after 5 years. In either case, the odds are against the entrepreneur, and no data or strategies demonstrate that leisure-based businesses have better odds.

There Are No Guarantees

Have you heard the claim, "This business can't fail"? Of course, neither could Mighty Casey, who, as the poem says, struck out. Leisure-based businesses are subject to the same limits and problems as any other kind of business. Of course, they require adequate capitalization, a carefully assessed market, access to clients and suppliers, competent bookkeeping, and well-chosen staffing. All kinds of issues may bring down even a good concept in a good location. However, leisure businesses have that added warning factor that "no one has to do it."

Warning

People begin an activity and then drop it for many reasons: inertia, time, lack of companions, skill hurdles, distance, and so on. However, there is another big reason related to recreation businesses: cost. Walking is free, downhill skiing is not. Research on flying shows that cost is the major factor in stopping 80% of those who begin lessons from getting a license.

Question: For what other recreation activities is cost central to continuation?

The other side of the failure issue stems from the same source. Enthusiasm may spring from personal experience. However, really liking the activity offered by a start-up does not always translate into success. There is always the downside of the activity life cycle. There are cost factors including the distribution of income in a catchment area and family composition in which those expensive additions—children—limit expenditures on recreation. Additionally, there is the source of information. If the claims of great expectations come from those promoting their equipment, franchise, or advice, then use caution before investing. If those promising success will benefit from your investment, ask questions, some of which follow.

First, what is the basis of projected markets? Again, there are no straight-line forecasts. I am amazed how often self-credentialed expert consultants base their recommendations on projections that continue current patterns. For example, a tourism and second-home island hired experienced consultants to develop plans for its ferry company, airport, and new school. All three consultants based their plans on straight-line population increases despite clear limits on waterfront development, market-cost parameters, demographic realities, and other factors, and that was without the recession that emerged in hard-hit Michigan. We will return to realistic assessment of potential markets several times. Here let it suffice that *there are always limits*.

Second, are there ways to beat the odds? For those who want to challenge themselves, I recommend the 2011 book *Thinking Fast and Slow* by Daniel Kahneman (Nobel Prize for economics in 2002). It is surprisingly engaging reading, perhaps because Kahneman is a behavioral psychologist, not an economist. However, for those not ready to take on the 481 pages, this book adopts several of his insights and perspectives. The theme is simple: Certain habits of making decisions commonly lead to mistakes. To compound the problem, those mistakes are most frequent when people are pretty sure of themselves. The solution? Informed and critical thinking.

Kahneman (2011) refers to countless studies that lead to the conclusion that there are two types of decision making, which he calls System 1 and System 2. System 1 refers to how people make most of their decisions most of the time, that is, quickly, often because they have to be made quickly. My usual example from flying is the unexpected and sudden entrance into zero visibility conditions requiring an immediate switch to instruments and a decision as to the best course for getting out. Experience, rather than flight manuals, provides the basis for the necessary action, generally made correctly by those who are "old, not bold" pilots.

System 1 does not identify all relevant knowledge, calculate validity of information, and complete a reasoned cost–benefit analysis and risk assessment. For most of life, it does not have to. For business decisions with long-term consequences, System 2, which completes all those operations, should be employed. Also, System 2 is required for criticizing and improving decisions that begin with System 1. The problem is that "System 2 is lazy." Most often, we have to make a real effort to employ System 2. (For example, reading this book.)

Perhaps surprisingly, both are relevant for this book. Understanding System 1 is useful for understanding many leisure choices for potential clients and how to shape them. System 2 is necessary if the recreation provider is to have a business that develops in ways that find and satisfy target markets. A number of perspectives, unique or at least especially significant for a recreation business, help recreation providers beat the odds.

Errors to Avoid

WYSIATI—What You See Is All There Is

The first error to avoid, according to Kahneman (2011), is WYSIATI— what you see is all there is. As with most of his themes, it is simple. The world is complex. A lot of disciplined effort is required for someone to ferret out all the relevant information on which to base an informed decision. So mostly people do a quick take on what they already see or think they know and then decide. It is tunnel vision that does not even see the tunnel. One common social-science slogan is, "it's a multivariate world out there." To make it worse, the world is an interactive system, and changes in one factor create changes in others. The world (in business, read "markets") won't hold still.

For example, say that 15% of the U.S. population over 17 plays golf. When assessing whether a new golf development will find a market, the investor can begin with a likely population catchment area. However, other factors could affect chances of finding a golf market. Only about 25% of those who report that they play golf are on a course once a month or more. Golf is relatively costly, so the investor has to factor in pricing against the considerable investment. There are economic factors of unemployment rates, income distribution, and area projections. Of course, the golf boom has leveled off, but it has the unique sports element of retaining a high percentage of older players. But some of them are moving south to gain a longer season, and so on and so on.

It is easier for investors to look at courses in the area to see if they are crowded and make a decision based on what they see or even the difficulty they had reserving a tee time last Saturday. Big elements such as recessions, the cost of gas, the impact of the housing market surplus on golf-based housing developments, and the participation trends that are not "straight line." After all, doesn't your enthusiasm count for more than all that complicated stuff?

Question: How Can This Go Wrong?

An experienced gambling resort company is seeking investors for a new project. It has identified a half dozen underserved markets in which to establish new casinos. You already know that gambling is a "money machine" for the operators, because all the odds favor the "house" and profit margins are built into the structure of the development and operation. Is this a surefire investment?

Clue: Look beyond what you see. It isn't all there is.

Further investigation of the industry will reveal a number of facts. First, all casinos do not succeed. Remote failing locations demonstrate the limits of the catchment area, mostly due to time and money travel costs. Second, there is new competition with online gambling opportunities and formats becoming readily available. Third, each location will have its own set of regulations and demands for revenue sharing. Fourth, it is difficult to start small when expectations for lavish venues are commonplace. Fifth, income and employment trends in the area may also limit the market. Some formats will tend to rule out the high-end market. All of these and other components of a System 2 decision are relevant.

What You Think You Know May Not Be Right

The second and corollary fallacy is that what you think you know may not be right. For example, a small tee-time sample may obscure that half the golf courses in the area are losing money or members or both.

As noted in Chapter 14 and elsewhere, many sources of data are available, often for free. But all of them require interpretation. Interpretation requires context analysis. Context includes several interacting elements.

Here we recognize the limits of personal perspectives. We all have limited experience. Probably more important, we view the world from a set of domain assumptions. These are so fundamental that for the most part we do not recognize their existence. We may believe that free enterprise always leads to growth. We may believe that everyone really wants to be in outdoor environments, or we may be sure that it takes competition to produce effort. Such assumptions are often too deep for us to recognize and evaluate.

Exercise

Again take your favorite or chosen recreation business concept. List all the relevant questions to which you do not know a well-supported answer. (A dozen ought to be easy.)

Sometimes we react with strong emotions to an observed action or even a single word without knowing why. We may have experienced a violation of how we define the world that rocks us to our core. That is, it challenges or even violates some domain assumption. Do we value schedule over flexibility, time at home over time with "the guys or girls," work over play, or regularity over spontaneity? Any of these may bias a business plan.

The problem is that these premises shape how we look at the world, what we see, and our mode of interpretation. We try to make sense of the behaviors of others out of our own worldview. In marketing, we project on others the same kinds of meanings and satisfactions we have found in certain environments, actions, or associations. So one of the purposes of social and behavioral science is to help us develop a more complete and critical understanding of why some people run to the point of exhaustion, enter strange and even threatening environments, or stay home and tend their gardens. In developing a recreation business, we need such enrichment and correction of our own understandings.

I Can Change the World

The third fallacy is the confidence that "I can change the world." The truth is that we can seldom change the behavior patterns of one person. Witness the common failure of basketball coaches, especially young ones who believe that their magic touch will transform the selfish, arrogant, and self-aggrandizing play of a pampered high school star into a mature college team player. Or the restaurant purchaser who is sure that she can make a success in a location with a string of failures.

The moral is simply that *past behavior is the best predictor of future behavior*. Of course, there are exceptions. Kids mature. A shrewd market analysis can sometimes create business success out of former failure. But the starting point for any thinking about leisure business is clear: What has been the history of such businesses? How do potential clients spend their time and money now? What are the most common traffic patterns in a city or resort area? With whom do target markets spend their non-work time?

This is why baseline numbers are a better jumping-off platform than hunches, flashes of insight, or the claims of enthusiasts. Of course, people do change . . . sometimes. However, if the success of a business dream requires changed behaviors, the entrepreneur needs to begin with current behaviors and then look critically at what may bring about change.

Moneyball

The fourth fallacy extolls why entrepreneurs need to learn to play moneyball. *Moneyball* is the title of a film extolling the wonderfulness of a real-life baseball general manager who, to oversimplify, largely ignored the expert judgment of scouts, managers, and coaches in selecting minor league players to nurture and advance in their system. The result was that a low-budget team won a lot of games and beat out the big spenders in the playoffs. (From my bias as a long-ago southpaw, it is important to note they had very good pitching.)

Kahneman (2011) uses this story to pound home the importance of base numbers. In the error of immediacy, decision-makers commonly ignore the numbers. Investment strategies should always begin with whatever data are available on what potential clients do now, where they do it, what they spend, and, when possible, what they do *not* do. Can a new opportunity alter those numbers? Of course, but certainly not always and only when something powerful overcomes inertia.

A correlate error is overgeneralization from small numbers. Localized data, one-time rather than trend numbers, and special cases may bias judgment. At the least, beginning with the numbers on potential client markets provides a base for developing realistic strategies. Current spending patterns suggest how allocations are made and where they might be altered. For example, average household spending on leisure has stayed at about 8 to 9% for decades. However, income levels and economic conditions produce limits. Strategies to change patterns begin with the present.

"Bayesian statistics," developed by an 18th century English clergyman, is a model of how people change decisions when confronted with evidence. An example is the likelihood that current participation in indoor fitness programs and measured dropout rates would be altered by a classy new facility. There are two bases in Bayesian probability analysis. The first is simply that the base (current) rates are *very* important. The second is that mathematical calculation of the impacts of a new factor is generally much lower than personal enthusiasms would produce. Anchoring judgment in base numbers is a necessary beginning. (More on this later.) Further, entrepreneurs need be critical of their own thinking and recall that System 2 is usually lazy.

Problems such as WYSIATI and overgeneralization from small numbers are common errors in business development. For example, "I have seen how those kids really love playing tennis and the parents I have talked to would love to see a professional developmental program available." Instead, entrepreneurs should ask how many kids and what else are they doing (baseline) and how much are most parents able and willing to pay and for how long (baseline).

Exercise

Pick a business and develop three critical questions to ask.

Clue: What would it take to change behaviors?

But doesn't the entrepreneur's judgment count for anything? Of course, in the end it is the entrepreneur's judgment that matters. After all, in most investment decisions, especially those in business start-ups, it is not "just money." This is the entrepreneur's life! As anyone who starts a business will note, especially at the retail service level, the demands on the entrepreneur's time, energy, and attention seem limitless. Probably these are aspects of the business that have appeal beyond profit. They may include location, association with congenial clients and staff, and the chance for entrepreneurs to do it their own way. Such side bets are not trivial.

Innovation vs. the Proven Market

Rafting wild rivers has been an activity growing in popularity. In fact, it has become so popular that the public managers of the now scarce resource, accessible white-water rivers, have often had to develop a permit system for allowing use of the resource. The issue of safety is also a concern. Left to themselves, many people will overestimate their skills and underestimate the necessary equipment for safe runs. This suggests that experienced personnel and good equipment are necessary for a viable business. But that is only the beginning.

"Entrepreneur A" began on one popular river in California and in time had operations in over six locations throughout the West. Staff were trained in established locations and then moved to others. The owner-manager became expert is assessing rivers and desirable campsites, pullouts, and seasons. In time, the company became known as a standard for the activity with national advertising and enormous investment. (Again, check websites. Try Salmon River Rafting and Rogue River Rafting.)

However, the managers went one step further. Listening to clients, they decided that there were two levels of rafters. One wanted the experience at reasonable cost. The other wanted a higher level of service and comfort. So the company offers two styles: one safe and simple and the other "gourmet" in food, comfort, staff support, and personal attention. The gourmet rafters pay at least a 50% premium for the higher level of service.

"Entrepreneur B" on the famous Rogue River in Oregon went the other way. That company offers 1-day rafting trips for those who want the experience at minimum cost. Then it expands into 2 and 3 days with camping and 3 days with nights in lodges for those unwilling or unable to sleep on the ground. However, recognizing that much of the plan was based on experience with that one river, the company stayed right on the Rogue, knowing its markets and the resource.

Question: Which strategy appeals to you most? Why? In the end, both are successful, so what are the criteria for deciding for or against expansion and diversification?

What Will the Remainder of This Book Attempt?

First, the book will attempt to improve the odds of recreation providers. Most fundamental, the book offers perspectives that can help providers to optimize the experiences of those who are paying for their services.

Second, the book provides useful material on what motivates players, possible clients, to make leisure-oriented decisions. Call it marketing or call it understanding people; it may translate into attracting clients.

Third, the book delves into a bit of System 2 strategy. A good attorney can offer advice about how *not* to "bet the farm," your home, or your retirement savings. The protections of incorporation and using OPM (other people's money) can reduce the personal risk. Currently, more and more businesses are being organized as limited liability corporations or limited liability partnerships. State rules and regulations change, so consulting a neighborhood or business consultant may help new entrepreneurs make a "formation" decision.

In the early 2000s, Western economies were deep into a recession that ended only after a partial recovery, another dip, and then a new plateau of moderate economic growth. In the recession, many recreation businesses failed, vacation and resort properties took major hits in value, and investment sources were limited. It is impossible to predict or time these economic ups and downs. However, for a new business, there are no easy times, so let's begin developing strategies that are realistic about obstacles.

The Major Project

Being somewhat skeptical of the value of exams about facts from the text and lectures, I suggest that students produce a major piece of original work during the term (a project which ought to work with a classroom or online format). Because recreation businesses are so varied, and because strategies and markets vary by location, I suggest that students begin early in the term to develop a business plan for the opportunity that excites them. Some or all of the plans, submitted in draft before the end of the term, may be presented in a class for all to examine and critique. This may be done in at least three stages, each of which can include a written assignment and a brief class presentation:

1. Select the business, begin to gather relevant material online and in visits to existing enterprises if possible, and outline likely markets. Include an analysis of current census data (online) for the proposed catchment area.

2. Outline a business plan to locate what is missing and produce a timetable for filling in the needed information and analysis.
3. Write the plan, allowing for enough time to refine and edit. (Good writing is a valuable resource in almost any job, especially writing clearly and concisely. Investors are unlikely to fund bad writers.)

The plan for an activity center that follows can be adapted to other types of businesses. It is aimed toward potential investors. Therefore, it should be exciting as well as informative, compelling as well as complete. (In some cases, a bank or start-up funding group will have its own format to follow.)

Activity Center Business Plan

I. The Concept:
- **Product or service description**
- **Relation to current resources**

II. The Market Area
- **Description of population**
- **Analysis of current recreation resources**
- **Data on current recreation participation and trends**

III. The Project
- **Full description of program, facilities, equipment, staffing, and scheduling**
- **Project differentiation: analysis of relationships to current public and planned public and market sector recreation opportunities**
- **History of similar or parallel projects elsewhere**

IV. Market Potential
- **Current participation base in market area**
- **Indications of potential growth**
- **Competition**
- **Market segmentation: age, gender, time scheduling, location**
- **Pricing factors**
- **Promotion plan**
- **Analysis of projected market growth**

V. Investment
- Cost of space
- Cost of equipment
- Personnel costs
- Operating expenses: summary or pro forma statement
- Taxation factors
- Initial capitalization requirements and sources of investments
- Start-up and 5-year projected financing needs
- Cash flow and break-even analysis
- Sources of income

VI. Formation
- Form of business
- Ownership and legal liability
- Assets and loan securities

VII. The Future
- Graphics of projected participation and income
- Timetable for beginning operations

VIII. Personnel
- Credentials and experience of principals in the project
- Résumés of advisers and consultants

Does this seem daunting? Of course. In a way, it is intended to be. Starting a successful business is more than announcing and opening the doors. All of the business plan elements ought to be considered first. Of course, neither in this exercise nor in real life will all of this material and analysis be available or possible. Nonetheless, every element is fair game for the loan officer or start-up specialist that the recreation provider is trying to convince. Repeatedly pleading ignorance will usually produce a rejection. But if the business is to be self-financed, the business plan is still a good outline of the issues that the recreation provider ought to address to maximize the chances of success.

CHAPTER 6:
INVESTMENT STRATEGIES FOR TOUGH TIMES

For new businesses, all times are tough in some ways.

Does B School Have the Answers?

Of course, conventional business and entrepreneurship analysis has a lot of wisdom that is not to be ignored. There are marketing techniques that have been successful. There are accounting practices that reveal problems. Failure to do good bookkeeping can land investors in the hot seats of the Internal Revenue Service and other taxing agencies. For some business functions, no amount of excitement or personal experience can make up for careless business practices.

However, most conventional analyses I have seen locate the failure of new businesses in the lack of money. That is, *undercapitalization* causes new businesses to run out of operating capital when markets develop more slowly than anticipated. It is true, of course, that instant markets are unusual and stable markets take time to nurture. So a realistic assessment of capital needs is necessary.

There is, on the other hand, another perspective on this issue. A business in trouble fails to attract and hold enough paying clients. For whatever reasons, the experience or product fails. Sometimes the root cause is in the concept, location, or some other foreseeable factor or combination of factors. In other cases, the business fails to provide an experience that is satisfying enough to retain clients and prompt them to bring along their friends. Person-to-person recommendations of current clients is the best form of promotion . . . and the lowest cost form.

Are There More Unconventional Factors for a Leisure Business?

Failure to Understand the Product

Remember, we are not selling a slightly improved microwave or more durable shoes here. All a recreation business (RB) has to sell is the experience. Therefore, promotion that is primarily comparative is unlikely to attract new players. Rather, in an RB, promotion has to focus on the quality of the experience, whether it be thrill, comfort, companions, the environment, or learning. Therefore, knowing research on satisfactions and motivations is crucial.

Failure to Recognize the Unique Character of Leisure

For the moment, review Rules 1 to 9.

!

Question

Try to identify at least one example out of your own experience as a client for each rule.

Hint: Some experiences may not have been ones you wanted to continue.

Failure to Think It Through

For example, if no one has to do it, then the competition may be out of sight. In usual marketing calculation, the competition is usually another supplier of a similar product or service. In an RB, the competition may be almost anything that is available and may promise some form of enjoyment or satisfaction. Reading may replace a hike, an online game, a movie, a shopping mall, or a park. Further, change is everywhere, as will be explored later in this chapter. Markets won't hold still.

Avoid System 1 Errors: The Halo Effect

Daniel Kahneman (2011) demonstrates how the System 1 mind can be primed either positively or negatively by a word or two, a recollection of an event, or association with a warm and friendly companion. This priming produces a *halo effect* that can influence a person's judgment on a current or anticipated experience. Obviously such priming is useful in designing promotional materials and advertising strategies. However, it can also lead to evaluations that are overly positive. For example, recalling a valued companion before assessing a leisure service may skew a person's judgment toward a false positive. The halo effect can be partly corrected by employing the Moneyball strategy of getting baseline numbers or getting a wide sampling of other users and clients.

Is Anything Important Simple?

Probably not, and certainly not an investment analysis. There are countless examples:

- A different location may also have a different set of cultures in the sought-after market.
- Weather aberrations can severely reduce visitors to a vacation area.
- Media attention to a new game or activity may prime a positive bias and evaluation. This has been called the "Olympics effect," for example as related to women's gymnastics or women's soccer. In both cases, some of the effect was temporary.
- Economic growth may involve gains in productivity relying on longer hours and greater pressure on the worker.

Numbers are important, but markets are more than numbers. As the following chapter examines, there are many cultural and stylistic elements in leisure choices. Everyone male between the ages of 65 and 74 cannot be simply profiled as to favorite activities or satisfactions even if most males do watch sports on TV.

Observation is a valuable approach to understanding what people do in relation to a particular resource and how they do it. For example, there may be more resting, socializing, and shopping than skiing at a resort that advertises its challenging ski slopes and powder snow. However, what we see is not all there is. Seeing what people do on-site may tell us little about the home-based worlds where they decide whether to go to the recreation site. Histories of activity and skill investment are largely hidden and may be difficult to access. The point is that people are not just skiers, golfers, swimmers, or anything labeled by an activity. That is, they have both constraints and alternatives.

The Big World, or Why Macro-Economics Is Important

This is not the place for a detailed analysis of economic models. However, the big picture of economic shifts, trends, and processes affects every kind of business. Globalization, recession, recovery, dislocations of production, distribution of income and wealth, scale of retailing (big-box stores), distribution patterns (logistics, online orders, and subcontracting), the rise of online shopping, and media shifts (from newspapers to the Web), all of these and other big-picture factors affect even local business. The larger economic movements affect financing, markets, costs of products, branding, and other local functions.

There are also political macro-changes. In the United States, an administration that invests heavily in environmental protection and natural resources for outdoor recreation may be followed by one that seeks to minimize government involvement in such areas. Such policies can make a difference in the quality and attractiveness of the resources that draw clients for secondary businesses.

Then there is the reality of recession. By definition, discretionary spending may be cut or even eliminated in household budgets when there are reductions in household income. Increases in unemployment ripple through regions and nations with drastic effects on leisure spending, both big ticket and immediate. Boats are abandoned rather than purchased. More vacations are taken in the car. Expensive opportunities are postponed. Even gambling is reduced by over 20%.

Issue

In the household you know best, what significant changes in income or necessary expenses have caused spending shifts? Did the increase or loss alter recreation spending?

Income and Wealth Define Markets for Leisure

As mentioned, the average of 8 to 9% of household income spent on leisure remained fairly consistent until about 1990. Then it crept upward only to be reduced by recession-related cutbacks. However, that is an average, either a mean or a mode. The distribution is another matter. The familiar bell-shaped curve applies here, as it does to all distributions. Some households spend almost nothing on leisure, usually due to low incomes or cultural prohibitions. Others with higher incomes and wealth may spend 50% or more on leisure broadly defined. If the leisure space and equipment of homes, upscale travel with luxury and privacy, designer play togs, and "big toys" such as yachts and cruisers, vintage sports cars, lavish entertaining, and third homes in exotic locales are included, then the 50% figure may be low. Many of the wealthy are little affected by recession. Some are affected, but spend anyway out of their surplus. The point is that shifts in income and wealth, not just unemployment and poverty, help define RB markets.

In assessments of business opportunities, the lure of high-end markets is hard to overestimate. The lifestyles of the rich and famous provide images of big spending that translate into big markets, or it seems. It is true that recessions seem to have little effect on the leisure spending of the wealthy. There are always hundreds of expensive yachts for sale. However, most luxury tours and resorts do not close in tough times. The problem with concentrating a business plan on high-end markets is, of course, saturation. Others have noticed that the markets, although small in number, have held up well in a recession. Also, the very wealthy, the upper 1% or even 10% in income and wealth, may be less likely than those on a tight pleasure budget to cut every possible expense corner. Having noticed this, upscale resort developers pile investment on investment, and many find bankruptcy in saturated markets.

At the other end, the officially poor, as measured by the very inaccurate household income levels that omit life circumstances such as persistent health problems and debts, are generally ignored in RB investment strategies. More recently, recession and unemployment have caused the government to discover a new category of those with very small discretionary incomes. Called the "near poor" and including the low-income working poor, this new category added to the officially poor constitutes up to 45% of the population. Their lives are precarious, less than three months from destitution if income is severely reduced or expenses are raised by an emergency. It does not mean that this enormous population segment is not interested in play, recreation, and diversion. But it does suggest that dollars spent will be limited and usually rationed carefully. An RB seeking new markets in the near poor will be competing with television and big-box shopping, not a luxury tour or big toy.

Of course, recreation providers can respond to the half of the population between the high and low by cutting costs. The danger is that the quality of the experience will also be reduced, which makes repeat visits or trips less likely. Perhaps the biggest challenge for leisure entrepreneurs is finding ways to offer a quality experience at limited cost. (More on this later.)

Government policies are also relevant here. Discretionary income is after-tax income. Levels of taxation in relation to income can shift spending. A major move from a progressive income tax to a VAT or consumption tax might make potential clients think twice about an expenditure. Dropping tax deductions on second homes would affect many vacation areas. Luxury taxes on expensive boats, or any boats over 15 feet long, would affect sales.

Tough Problem

What RB opportunities might find viable markets among lower income markets? How can they be marketed in a way that did not appear to be condescending or even discriminatory?

Nothing Lasts ... Except Change

No one has to be reminded of the power of technologies to change even ingrained habits related to recreation. The telephone made arranging events from household to household more convenient. The elevator created skyscrapers. The car gave flexibility to travel. The jet opened long distances to vastly expanded markets. Television transformed time use in almost every home. Now there is the home computer; online everything; and portable devices with new programs, apps, and connections almost every month. Clearly, all of these devices and websites are not just for communication, information, and business. They are the new "sites" for fun, play, and leisure. The difference is that the opportunities go almost anywhere with the bearer.

How will all of the online stuff affect the leisure investments of time and money? Frankly, no one knows for sure. The enthusiasts claim that everything will change. The cautious argue that deeply ingrained habits do not change that easily, at least for those over age 25 and certainly for those big markets of those over age 65.

How large is the online experience market? In a decade, the Web has almost eliminated local travel agencies, as even remote bed and breakfasts have websites. Technology has expanded the market reach of bed and breakfasts. It has not put them out of business. Some technologies enhance opportunities for other businesses. Remember how the interstate highway system, the car, and now the internet replaced old hotels with motel chains? The good news is that technologies have enabled all sorts of new RB opportunities. The bad news is that competition is no longer just local.

Question

What new technology will most affect leisure? Will its impacts open more businesses than it closes?

Clue: How will it change (or not) how people live day to day? On special occasions?

Personal: How much time do you spend texting? What do you do less of because of this time use?

Resistance to Change

Kahneman (2011) calls attention to the endowment error. It operates on the behavioral level. By and large, people whose leisure is sedentary

---

do not become physically active due to a new opportunity or activity. They continue watching television. Cultural patterns tend to change slowly, if at all.

However, the endowment error can also be a problem for businesses. A gradual erosion of a market may be unnoticed or explained away by an entrepreneur deeply invested in a particular activity base or locale. For example, if the owner of a camping site for RVs, trailers, and various campers sees his trade eroding, does he analyze changes in travel patterns, equipment investments, and the characteristics of his visitors, or does he just put up a couple of new billboards, assuming the market is still unchanged?

Endowment in the form of personal loyalty, habit, or unquestioned assumptions may cause bad judgment. Change is constant.

The next chapter looks more closely at trends and fads. Here we note a seeming contradiction: Change is everywhere, and people don't change much. How can we reconcile that no market remains the same with the fact that past behavior is the best predictor of future behavior? (Is it a cop-out to suggest that to begin to deal with this dilemma, the reader may find it helpful to read the remainder of this book?)

Here we note a few obvious perspectives: Everything new isn't promising, but almost nothing lasts indefinitely. There are bad trends such as long- and short-term fuel prices and good trends such as people being able to compare opportunities and products online. There are indications that some personal recreation investment and involvement is not only accepted but applauded in the formerly work-oriented society. Note the way retirees build their timetables and friendships around their leisure lives. My own experience with undergraduates who write scenarios of what they hope their lives will be like suggests that leisure will be central to their value and investment systems. On the other hand, economic insecurity can dash many hopes and expectations.

Issue

Look around. How has Walmart affected local business? How has online purchasing affected big-box retailing? What change is next? Is there any such thing as local loyalty?

Jumping to Conclusions

Let Kahneman's (2011) warning suffice: System 1 decision making can be costly. System 2 thinking is lazy. It calls for gathering of relevant data, critical analysis, and weighing salience. It is neat and exciting to promote an innovation. It makes us feel advanced and efficacious: We are making a difference. Stressing newness may also be a good marketing theme.

On the other hand, promoting a new opportunity is most likely to be successful when it can be associated with old satisfactions. Chapter 14 examines leisure experience more closely to identify what really turns people on. New possibilities of old meanings would seem to be a good formula.

In the meantime, in newness, it is important to remember price. It may be true that money cannot buy happiness, but lack of money can rule out of consideration some attractive opportunities. New is good, but there are always limits.

With these warnings, let's move on to identifying potential markets and what is most likely to prompt the investment of those scarce resources of money and time.

CHAPTER 7:
TARGET MARKETS

Markets are, after all, what it is all about. No market, then no business. Many seemingly good ideas do not lead to successful businesses. Again, there is no fixed and clearly identified market for what no one has to do. However, good ideas can not only find but also create markets. For a recreation business, how?

It Is New: Is It a Trend or a Fad?

To begin, there is the activity life cycle. Again, no activity will have sustained growth that keeps on increasing in participants. However, some will gain a plateau, usually something below its peak, that provides a basis for profitable business development. Figures 7.1 and 7.2 illustrate this.

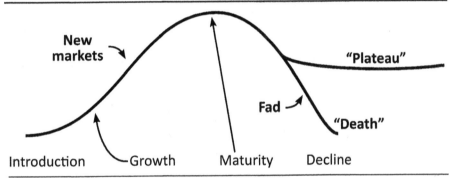

Figure 7.1. Product life cycle curves.

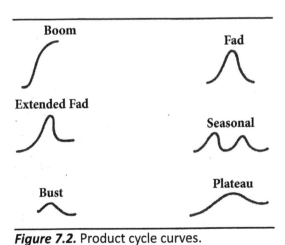

Figure 7.2. Product cycle curves.

A Fad or a Sustainable Plateau
Requires Careful Analysis

A fad, often referred to in the media as a craze, gets a lot of attention, has a rapid growth period, and then fades into obscurity. An activity cycle that provides a good market possibility has a decline from its growth peak to a sustained plateau level. A growth pattern in the early phase often catches investment enthusiasts in overestimating potential markets.

> ### Research
>
> Think of examples for each of the product life cycle types in the Figure 7.2? Analyze one and why it succeeded or failed.

The big question is, how can we distinguish a viable trend from a fad? To begin, we consider the source. Some will have a financial interest in promoting an activity as "the wave of the future." Those who are promoting products, franchises, and consulting are likely to underestimate the potential decline once initial enthusiasm is exhausted. They gain from being unrealistic. At the same time, some get caught up in the activity and are sure that everyone will find it as engrossing as they do. For example, considerable media attention was given to a new manufactured activity that requires the construction of an expensive set of walls and surfaces, the development of extremely demanding physical skills, and a high injury risk. Further, it would be limited to a young athletic market. Its chances for becoming a good investment? We already know. Most racquetball courts are now fitness centers.

Second, we consider the possibility of parallel innovations. Why is this game, implement, or venue better than others that are competing for the same target market? At this point, all of the usual factors of cost, geographical and skill accessibility, and attractiveness come into play. If an innovation is that exciting, it is likely that there will be similar developments, the Hula Hoop being an exception that tests the rule, or was it?

Third, we need to be realistic about market segments. In sports, for example, there are large drops in participation in two life-course periods: school-leaving age when opportunities and social rewards fall and around age 45 when physical demands may lessen satisfaction and, for some, family demands compete for time. (This is when softball players become Little League coaches.) We'll further examine evaluating target markets, but here we'll just stop with the warning.

Fourth, and this is *very big*, how does the activity fit into current patterns of behavior? For example, videos, DVDs, Netflix, Fire, and now streaming have expanded and enhanced what most people were doing already. People did not have to make great changes to their habits or priorities to adopt these new technologies. On the other hand, becoming a private pilot requires great investments of disciplined learning away from home and on other people's schedules, as well as thousands of dollars in expense. It should not seem surprising that the number of beginners completing pilot training to even the first-level license is decreasing.

Two rules are important here: past behavior is the best predictor of future behavior and look at the baseline numbers. A close examination of who the new participants are in age, gender, resources, and culture is also important. Two historical cases may remind us of predictions gone wrong.

Cases

Case 1: The Video Game Parlor

Those who are old enough may remember when new video electronic game parlors sprang up all over the country. Their enthusiasts called them a can't-miss growth investment opportunity. Those who were skeptical saw some simple facts: (1) They required going to an away-from-home site where access to the game of choice was not assured. (2) Most important, a high proportion of the market was preteen and early teen males who were prone to faddish enthusiasms, had limited spending money, and who became a year older every 12 months. Then the new technologies of at-home gaming consoles and home computers made the trip to the emporium unnecessary. At the same time, the major market segment aged, got bored, or moved on, which left a rather low plateau for the specialized parlor. The limited market segment was easy to recognize. Aware "techies" would have anticipated the new competition.

Case 2: Racquetball

Somewhat further back, there was the can't-miss new sport of racquetball. Played first on the often vacant squash courts on campuses and then growing with dedicated facilities, it seemed an everyone-is-doing-it activity to those in the somewhat nearsighted higher education world. Recognizing that those playing as students would need off-campus opportunities when they entered the then growing economy, clubs were built, especially in urban locales, and for a time, many did well.

The sport was thought to be especially appealing because it was easy to learn and could be coed. The short-handle racquet made it easier to hit and control than did a tennis or squash racquet. Further, the relatively small court space could offer a winter racquet experience for summer tennis players. However, in a matter of a few years, a high proportion of these clubs closed or were turned into multiactivity fitness centers. Some entrepreneurs were glad they had not literally set the walls in concrete.

What happened? Paradoxically, the relative ease of gaining beginner skills seemed to work against long-term commitment. As we will analzye in Chapters 10 and 14, the matching of skill and challenge is central to satisfaction in activity such as sports. If the challenge of the short handle becomes too low as skill is gained, then the result is boredom. This was one factor in the failure of the businesses to attract many dedicated tennis players in the winter. The carryover was inadequate. Further, the market segment was limited by access, cost, work schedules, and competing attractions for too many of those who had left the campus for the world of work.

Foreseeing all of this would have required a more sophisticated analysis than most entrepreneurs are capable of doing. Further, estimating how many racquetball players would live or work within a viable distance from the facility would have been complex. However, the tale does illustrate how an adequate analysis would have been multifactorial and interactive.

Exercise

Analyze a current craze using Figure 7.1. For example, what might be the future of senior soccer or senior softball? List pro and con factors including location, seasonality, baseline numbers, and physical limits. What outdoor sports or activities offer better markets?

Hint: Begin with real numbers, costs, and location, if possible.

Other Questions

Before leaving this perennial issue for a time, we put forth a few questions about the activity cycle problem.

- How much would most people have to change their habits and life investments to adopt the new possibility?
- Is it possible to estimate from the current growth pattern the potential size of the market for the new experience?
- In what ways can you avoid jumping to conclusions, falling for the halo effect, and being critical of the claims of enthusiasts besides recollecting that the media seek the unusual, not the ordinary?
- How can you distinguish good trends from bad trends? For example, the good trend of increased interest in recreation in natural environments may be countered by the bad trends of increased fuel prices and decreased government investment in resource maintenance, and crowding.
- What are the underlying trends in discretionary income? For example, if health care costs go up, will recreation spending go down and for whom?

Whoever said life was simple?

Probabilities and Personal Judgment

Fortunately, we don't have to choose one and ignore the other. A famous Fidelity Funds manager used to recommend that potential investors find stores, services, and products they really liked and then explore investment opportunities. That's good advice for leisure-based investment as well. Especially with franchise development, checking it out, talking to the owner and front-line employees, and watching the clientele can be a useful first step. But it is only a beginning.

Exercise

It may be a good time to get back out into the field. Interview the manager of what appears to be a successful RB with questions raised in the text above. No reading can substitute for real-world investigation. The danger, of course, is that personal enthusiasm and that of those invested may overwhelm System 2 analysis.

> **Question**
>
> How might leisure business investments be especially vulnerable to System 1 decisions?
>
> **Clue:** Check the possible bias of first impressions and those who are newly engaged.

Big Markets: What Most People Do a Lot

Too late! Television retailing is already oversaturated so that profit margins are tiny and competitors are behind every big-box storefront and website. The same may be true for other mass-market leisure items. Breaking into the growing mid-market motel business means competing with proven brands with access to capital. I remember talking with the young owner of an attractive motel within sight of a major cross-country interstate who was trying to gain clientele. The problem was that the chains with their known prices and quality had most travel units prereserved online before they saw his attractive business. However, on-line sites now stress quality ratings that include the local enterprises.

Are there openings for services in the big-numbers markets, even considering the 80–20 rule? One possibility is location. A careful investigation in convenient locations of camping opportunities, equipment sales and service, specialty guiding and tour arranging (especially in backcountry), animal care and boarding, or some other facilitation for a large market may reveal an opportunity. However, we must first know the market area numbers, travel patterns, and visitor numbers and goals.

> **Question**
>
> For which recreation provisions may higher quality capture markets underserved by former providers or create new markets?
>
> **Example:** Which youth sports provide such an opportunity, especially in this day of single-sport specialization and year-round engagement? Do for-profit programs augment or compete with public and school sports programs? What about cost exclusions due to high fees and expenses?
>
> **Alternatives:** Private programs that augment school music and arts offerings are taken for granted, yet advantage young musicians and artists whose families can afford individual instruction. Are sports any different? (Does anyone question that athletic aptitude is independent of household income?)

Another possibility is quality. Current providers may have begun with a poor design, failed to upgrade or maintain, had too many incompetent staff, or not understood what the target market wanted in an experience. Some markets invite competition.

A third opportunity is based on new development. A destination natural resource or activity offering may have opened, expanded, or improved its market draw. Such change can also open possibilities for auxiliary businesses. More on public–private synergy later, especially Chapter 8, but it pays to watch what the public sector agencies are or are not planning and financing.

Cases

Case 1: Location and Innovation

On the Oregon coast near a park with dunes and a small lake, an attractive private campground met a market opening when the entrepreneur saw that the public facilities were full and reserved a high percentage of the time. However, clients came for a very special ocean-and-dune experience and demanded quality. Then a secondary business developed renting equipment.

Case 2: A New Market!

A new activity was developed using the same resource (i.e., the dunes). Climbing and then running or falling down the dunes has been overwhelmed by a new technology. Sand surfing began with smaller surfing or boogie boards. Then businesses developed better boards—faster, lighter, and more controllable. So two businesses took off: equipment design and manufacture, and on-site rental and instruction. What would come next? There are other dunes along the coast that are not in public parks, seashores, and play areas. Here is the question: Would it be more profitable in the long run for an entrepreneur to buy or lease a dune site and develop a business there or to stay with the established resource that would be maintained by the state or feds?

Line up arguments for each strategy: controlling private land or expanding a business using the public site. There are several elements in such a debate including investment cost, quality, control, and long-term growth. Which has the greatest profit potential? Which has the greatest risk?

Some markets are saturated. Reading a list of high-end luxury lodging businesses at burgeoning Park City, Utah, raises the question of how many people want to spend $700 to $1,500 a night for a room plus hundreds for a meal. (And that does not take a snowless December into account.) Some product markets are saturated due to the website retailers that now offer "free" (i.e., included in the price) shipping to the customer's door. No checkout lines, parking and traffic issues, or finding items sold out.

> ## Clue
>
> Examine the household composition and trends of your market area. It's free! The U.S. Census breaks down all sorts of population numbers so you can estimate numbers of adult singles, gender, children, income, education, and other target market designations. Big markets may be underserved, especially as populations change.

A study of a changing area in suburban Chicago some years ago revealed two important factors. First, the population was aging and increasingly single. That is, fewer children and more adults, especially women, looking for activity outside of their apartments. Second, a fairly new freeway cut off easy access to a proposed activity center from a large residential area. Such change both opened and closed markets for relevant activity offerings.

Missing the Target

As just suggested, populations can change, in geographical areas and within populations. Such change can create underserved markets. A few commonplace examples follow:

- The active old is one underserved market. In the United States, people are living longer and in better health. Further the word is out that staying active physically, mentally, and socially tends to prolong health and life satisfaction. Of course, this is hardly new information. I did an analysis of such markets for a major consulting firm, Battelle International, decades ago that stressed expanding opportunities and support for what older people were already doing. Retirement villages advertising their range of activities (and downplaying that their residents get older and more infirm eventually) are a multibillion-dollar business sector. Nonetheless, if we recognize that most older people "retire in place" rather than relocate, we may find possible markets for activity and services.

- The proportion of households made up of single adults is rising fast. Most are employed and want to get out of the apartment and be engaged with others who have similar leisure orientations. Note that at least half are women who seek both social interaction and safety.
- Often stereotypes related to age ("Generation whatever"), cultural background, and income level prevent the discovery of potential markets. All stereotypes are not wrong, but many miss the variety of interests within an identified population segment. This raises some doubt about market segment analysis based on styles (usually labeled with cute acronyms) that may overgeneralize from identifiers such as education level, housing type, neighborhood, and ethnicity.

Niche Markets and Leisure Subcultures

The other end of the big markets that are based on what most people do most of the time are the niche markets. They are the .5 of 1% markets in participation. Establishing numbers and trends is difficult because the baselines are so small. Identifying development possibilities is limited by the fact that the activities seldom appear on any of the household and census surveys. Nonetheless, those who know the activity well and can locate in a strategic spot have developed profitable businesses. Now the internet provides a new means of contacting niche markets widely dispersed. For example, a craftsman who hand-built custom bows and arrows in Xenia, Ohio, for decades in a mail-order format with specialty magazine classified ads now could reach a potential world market with a website.

These niche markets have been called leisure subcultures in the social science literature. They are formed informally and through narrowly focused organizations based on a specialty activity. Examples are literally endless: from a needlework style to Native American archaeology, from rattlesnake hunting to chamber music, from poetry writing to scaling 12,000-foot mountain peaks. Some are local. Some bring together widely dispersed residences. They do, however, have some common characteristics:

- They require a high level of skill development. According to Robert Stebbins, (1979) high-commitment amateurs' standards are much the same as professionals'.

- They tend to form associations of participants similarly dedicated who become their closest extrafamilial friends.
- They often play for pay as semiprofessionals whose major income is from another source. (There may be more semipro musicians than full-time professionals.)
- They schedule their lives and especially vacations around the activity.
- They are willing to invest disproportionate time and money in instruments, travel, and instruction to hone their skill.
- They attempt to transcend age boundaries for the activity, especially upper age norms.

Stebbins has studied amateur magicians, chamber music players, baseball players, and several other highly committed devotees of a central life investment. Some niche markets can occur almost anywhere. Some require specialized environments (e.g., high mountains, white-water rapids, backcountry landing strips, or a core group of theater performers and support workers). A few are high end in expenditures, such as rebuilding warbird airplanes, and some are low end, such as hand carving folk art objects. Some people sing opera, and some pick banjos. What they have in common is the centrality of the activity to their lives and their willingness to invest in raising their skill level. Some markets rely on location. A set of sheer rock faces 150 miles from an eastern metropolis can attract enough climbers to support a thriving business that includes supplies, equipment, repair, and instruction. Updrafts off hilly or mountainous slopes can attract enough of those rare birds, soaring pilots. Other specialty groups can form almost anywhere, because the primary requirement is a core base of participants. Woodworking and painting require no special environment, but they do require equipment, which can escalate in complexity and costs.

How do we discover such a market? For the most part, because they require a high understanding of the nature and requirements of the base activity, those likely to be successful in a business venture already know about possibilities. That is, they are already amateurs themselves. Nonetheless, careful analysis is still necessary. A devotion to an activity does not substitute for counting numbers and costs in a System 2 process.

Assessing Target Markets

Any market identification and analysis begins with behaviors. Who, where, when, and with whom are essential questions. To illustrate this process, we can outline an approach to it. For example, suppose you want to enter what you believe to be a market that is at least stable and could grow in an area with the right new business. Further, you would like to locate in or near the city where you have family and friends. How might you begin?

1. If, for example, your concept is for a fitness center, then first locate the competition. That would include not only any for-profit enterprises but also opportunities offered by public and not-for-profit organizations such as recreation districts, YMCAs and YWCAs, churches, synagogues, and neighborhood programs. Locate them carefully on a map of what you believe will be your catchment or market area. Then begin to explore siting that maximizes access and minimizes competition for your enterprise.

2. Do the numbers. Again, the most recent U.S. Census Bureau tract breakdowns are invaluable. If your business concept is sited and will rely at least in part on retailing, then a full analysis of who can get to the site and how conveniently is paramount.

3. Match the best participation data with the census demographics. This process is still only preliminary. One problem is that the best numbers on participation are too general, too old, or too expensive. However, at least it is possible at this point for you to eliminate gross errors. For example, you could evaluate a proposed bowling center by using the Statistical Abstracts trends on participation, estimating a continued decline, taking 25% of the total as the major market, and then looking at population figures for the adjacent census tracts. If it takes, for example, a population of 60,000 within a half hour's drive to provide a minimal base, then many locations are ruled out quickly. Then add in factors such as age and education distributions to further refine the potential market and competitive facilities. If the numbers still hold up, then further investigation may be warranted.

4. Fourth, you need to examine the same style of businesses in similar locations, to gain a sense of successful provisions and styles. For example, with bowling leagues generally losing clientele, additional offerings such as food and drink, entertainment, meeting space, and programming offset the losses.

5. At this point, you have a wealth of information and need to go fully into System 2. How viable are the target markets, or are System 1 biases blocking critical analysis? It is time for you to develop a full business plan and subject it to critical comment by others, including participants in the activity base and nonparticipants. It is not too early for a premortem. (See Chapter 14 for an introduction of this process.)

6. Be specific. The type of business has to be resolved into a particular business in a real location with planned promotion and distribution channels and resulting capitalization requirements. If you are to employ some percentage of OPM (other people's money), remember that your next presentation will be to professional skeptics such as bankers and possible investors. (Again, I have a bias from observation; don't bet the homestead, your kid's education, your retirement, or, especially, the savings of friends and relatives unless they are part of the business. If you can't sell it, take the warning.)

Project

If you have identified the business for which you will create a business plan, begin Steps 1 to 6 for your market study.

Numbers Are Not Everything

There is no substitute for getting the best base statistics possible. However, identifying target markets requires more than statistics. One approach is much more nebulous, but can be critical. We can call it style, culture, or preferences. The issue is that everyone does not have the same set of experiences, values, and learning. For example, in some cultures eating together is integral to almost any leisure event. In others, drinking after a sports occasion, after doing or watching, is inseparable from the activity. In some cultures, dancing means that everyone dances and in others it means they watch. What is classical in one culture is everyday or even folk in another. Styles of engagement may be boisterous and emotional in one culture or quiet and contained in another.

This cultural diversity can make operation of a leisure-based business in locations that draw from several cultures complex. Integration may be an ideal, but makes some clients uncomfortable. A simple example is a fitness club in which most younger clients prefer mixed-gender settings and socializing, whereas older clients, especially female, prefer a separated time and place. Another example is a swimming pool for which time must be scheduled for children, teens, and lap-counting senior fitness swimmers.

Case: Good Idea, but . . .

An interesting failure in terms of culture occurred in England over the last decade. An entrepreneur decided to build on the widespread phenomenon of literary tourism in that country. Mostly it refers to Joyce walks in Dublin, authors' homes refurnished in period modes and opened to the public, and tours of sites of books and plays by writers from Shakespeare to le Carré. This business concept was based on the work of England's most popular writer of novels, Charles Dickens. It was sited in the heart of Dickens country and called Dickens World. Great care went into the re-creation of streets, houses, prisons, poor houses, and other artifactual sites. After 10 years, it was evident that the project, although still open and struggling, had failed. No doubt many factors contributed to this failure, but I would suggest a cultural one. Those who read old novels, however popular, seldom embrace theme parks. In fact, it was literary lovers of Dickens who derided the entire idea.

Cultural elements are also significant for promotion. This is called market segmentation in business school. The elements of an experience that attract one market segment may turn off another. Look at an urban public beach. Many public recreation managers have had to set up zones for different kinds of activity, styles, or cultures. Beach volleyball does not mesh well with preschool children or older adults coming to read.

The point is that a business concept should include the styles of likely use. All of those included even in the committed 20 to 25% of all those who do an activity do not do it alike. As will be suggested further on, one key and often neglected form of market research is observation. Before succumbing to the sales pitch and ordering play equipment for a play area, we need to go see how kids actually play.

One More Big Clue in Marketing

A central factor, often *the* factor, in people enjoying a recreation experience is other people. In Chapter 14, we further examine what this suggests for the operation of a leisure site. For marketing, there are two major implications.

First, especially for a located business, the most important advertising is free. That is, it is what people tell other people—their family, friends, work associates, neighbors, and so on. Of course, this can also work against a business. Nothing kills a new restaurant quicker than negative personal reviews. The same is true for any business not selling a *Consumer Reports*–tested product, but an experience. Therefore, Chapter 13 on "Servicing the Experience" may be near the end of the book, but it is first in importance.

Second, Kahneman (2011) analyzes the significance of associations in decision making. For marketing, this suggests that promotional programs need to analyze the experiences related to the business and feature them in advertising or other promotions. It is no accident that advertising for tourist locales usually features attractive people (now of all ages up to 70) having fun. The promise of associations is central to choices. (I would add that the common use of celebrities may be the least effective advertising device. I doubt that recreational tennis players identify with the latest 18-year-old power hitter. However, if contemplating a vacation with tennis involved, they are attracted by a program that ensures association with compatible others.)

!

Question

What are the most important associational factors in promoting and managing an RB?

Hint: Observe multiple sites and times of day.

A Final Note on Bias

In the U.S. culture and economy, a couple of biases have at least a contextual impact on leisure businesses.

Work Bias

More than in the cultures of most developed economies, work is considered a wonderful thing in the United States and the very term *leisure* connotes laziness and sloth. In sociology, traditionalists who study work organizations, crime, and family have generally considered leisure as a topic unworthy of study. For decades, government research centers in Europe supported social science research into leisure; however, in the United States, use of the dreaded word guaranteed quick rejection by funding agencies.

More important, American cultural values have placed a low value on leisure. Recently there has been some change, as those with money, investment groups, and bankers have recognized the importance of the sector in the economy. My own research over the years has been consistent with studies that found that close relationships are most important to most people and their life satisfaction. Further, immediate communities, including families, find their expression, development, and consolidation to a great extent in leisure activity. Recreation is only slightly connected to work, but closely tied to people's central associations. More on this later, but note here that evidence is clear that European colleagues were far ahead of those in the United States in recognizing that leisure is not peripheral.

The bias is receding somewhat. Current emphasis on "successful" aging has directed greater attention to leisure activity. Literally hundreds of studies have found that when the prerequisites of adequate income and functional health are met, it is regular social, physical, and mental activity that marks those satisfied with later life. Some now even call it "leisure."

Let me repeat a story from the fourth edition of my text *Leisure*. Almost 20 years ago, sponsors convened the first major conference on Work and Family. The research reported on time conflicts and other issues, especially now that the majority of mothers are in the paid workforce. Women scholars largely conducted the research. My contribution was a paper suggesting that there is more to life than work and family and presenting some evidence on the significance of leisure, play, or whatever one prefers to call it. The paper was reprinted in the organization's newsletter, wherein some of the work–family experts presumably read it. Now, years later, the terminology, including conference title, has been changed to Work and Life. Probably my counterpoint had little direct influence, but the change is significant.

Capitalist Bias

The critical economist John Kenneth Galbraith (1958) pointed out 60 years ago that generally in capitalist economies there is an investment bias. It is simply that a disproportionate share of investment capital goes to the market sector rather than the public sector of schools, health services, national parks and forests, and the infrastructure that makes most business possible. There is an ideology that, despite evidence of overbuilding and bankruptcies, the market sector is always more efficient than the public sector. The obvious facts of inefficiencies everywhere, waste, and fraud throughout the economy seldom seem to threaten firmly held beliefs.

Not to belabor the argument, but I find there is an important way this bias affects RB investments. Consider the wide range of leisure-based businesses that depend on public programs and resources. Community sports, many arts programs, natural-resource-based activity, and school instruction and venues are direct and necessary public provisions. Highways and other transportation infrastructure, conservation of water and forest resources, safety and law enforcement, and so on provide indirect support. All of this requires capital in the form of public investment. (There is no movement to abolish the Coast Guard, only to reduce its funding. How can this affect water sports?) The point is simple: Those making leisure-based investments need to learn to support and work with the public sector.

We'll look at markets and marketing more. However, contexts are important as well.

CHAPTER 8:
A TIME AND PLACE

There is a long history of references to leisure time. Traditional economists, firmly believing in the primacy of work, have worked out a number of equations concerning the income–leisure time trade-off. Their assumption is that workers usually choose greater income rather than nonwork time. They see this as (surprise!) a rational decision process in which there is a tipping point at which workers see what money can buy as less valuable than time in which to spend and enjoy it.

Time as a Scarce Resource and Leisure as a Choice

Underlying the trade-off is the premise that there is such a thing as leisure time that is left over after work and maintenance tasks are completed. Especially in Europe, decades of research have been based on the same concept, that there is time free of requirements, which in various languages is called "free time." My argument is that there is no such thing or it is very rare. Further, the idea can be dangerous in the development of a leisure-based business.

The counterargument is simple. There is seldom, if ever, a time when everything else is completed. For many kinds of employment, operating a business being one, there are always uncompleted tasks. That is why we budget time as well as money. It is a scarce resource. One of the great surprises of most new retirees is that "I can't believe how busy I am!" and how many postponed tasks remain undone months and years into retirement. Research shows that time pressures are greatest for employed mothers, especially single mothers of preschool children. "Launching" when the last child leaves home changes but does not obliterate time pressures. You can pretty much figure out differences in time pressures yourself.

The point is that that "free time" is a myth. Leisure is not a leftover, but a decision. Engagement in leisure activity requires choosing priorities, allocating time periods, protecting against interference and counterpressures, and persisting in carrying out the choice. Leisure is not a residual quantity of time, but an allocation of a scarce resource. Of course, time is scarcer for some people than others.

There is also the counterargument that if time is scarce and precious, why do people spend so much time watching television? There is an answer. Most TV viewing, even some sports for fans, is low demand, low cost, available, habitual, and often erratic in attention. In any case, for a leisure business, marketing is attempting to provoke a choice of the use of scarce resources: time, money, and often energy. The question for the client is not, what do I do with this leftover time? But it is, is this opportunity valued and satisfying enough for the investment of scarce resources?

This brings us back to the fundamental assumption of leisure marketing and of this book: Selling a recreation experience requires that it promise more satisfaction than alternatives that have lower costs. Again, no one has to do it. It requires the potential client to make time. That is, recreation business will depend on decisions. They may be System 2 decisions and weigh costs, alternatives, and longer term outcomes, or they may be System 1 decisions and in more of a rush to judgment. In any case, they are a choice in a matrix of other possibilities and demands.

Recreation "Takes Place"

With the exception of daydreaming and fantasizing, both significant leisure, leisure has location. It may be conveniently located at home, or it may require a costly flight to some place special. However, residential space, and especially privacy, is not without cost. Attractive rooms and yards can be costly and, therefore, are the result of decisions about resources. "There ain't no free lunch . . . or leisure," or at least not much.

"Taking place" leads to a number of analytical approaches. First, tourism research has developed and revised the gravity model of leisure travel. It was deceptively simple at first. Inertia, staying where you are, is relatively cost free. Moving against the pull of gravity requires effort. The further the goal for travel, the greater the energy cost to overcome inertia. Therefore, greater distance requires greater payment in time, effort, and usually money.

Overcoming inertia from a dead stop calls for more energy than keeping moving once in transit. Therefore, the attraction pull of a leisure destination has to be strong enough to overcome initial inertia and then distance costs. For most choices, there may also be a limit on the time available that rules out certain distance possibilities.

The implication again is that people make decisions. The addition is that time and distance add measurably to the requirement that the anticipated experience be attractive enough to overcome those costs. The further implication, obviously, is that a recreation opportunity closer to its participant base is likely to do better.

The second analytical approach suggests that there are barriers around most locations. Mapping "as the crow flies" is not of much use, because we are not crows. For recreation venues relatively nearby, issues include public transportation; natural barriers such as rivers; constructed barriers such as freeways; barriers of perceived danger versus safety; and transportation-related barriers such as parking, convenience to customary travel routes, and rush-hour timetables.

Of course, all businesses have money costs. However, in many cases, the time and travel costs are greater for many potential clients. Credit cards alleviate the pressures of having enough cash on hand. Various payment plans can at least postpone the need for money. But time and distance are always there.

"If you build it, they will come" sounds neat in a movie, but don't count on it. (In fact, it seems that the real Field of Dreams movie site has had an activity life cycle.) If you build it in a location with high travel costs for potential clients, they often will not come, even to an attractive experience.

"Nearby" to potential clients as assessed through population analysis is a complement to any business plan. "On the way" to other destinations is a real convenience. Strip malls are ideal for some retailing and deadly for some activities. The moral is that location is too important to be left to accident or simple availability. It is central to any business strategy.

The third analytical approach asks, what can wealth buy? Of course, a lot of things. But in relation to leisure, there is a big one. It is privacy or space. It is well demonstrated that the really wealthy are willing to pay very high prices to avoid most of the rest of the population. Private country clubs may have a limited number of memberships costing up to a half million dollars and yearly dues and fees exceeding the average middle-class income. Resorts may be located on islands accessible only by private plane with only a few "cottages" or villas and high levels of service. The theme is privacy and limited access, with luxury important but secondary.

Luxury and quality of experience are not identical. Further, there are differences in tastes. The once exclusive and still expensive Rockefeller developments (RockResorts) were sited in major tracts of space with great natural beauty. Even the name connotes status and privacy. While there have been changes in their policies, they remain places where those who can pay can avoid the crowds for a price. Again, location,

location. Privacy alone is not enough. High-end opportunities also have to be designed and operated for an RB to offer a great set of experiences. But separated location is the beginning.

Question

What would be the ideal location for a particular RB? Which compromises are least damaging?

Clue: Who are the clients, and where are they?

Climate Is Also a Choice, Even if Weather Is Uncertain

The climate and weather issue is so obvious that it calls for little explanation. However, that does not make it unimportant.

The attractions are evident. For outdoor sports and activity, participants head south in the winter and north in the summer. For leisure, people escape limiting conditions and seek better environments. This simple fact creates leisure seasons. In turn, those seasons attract residents and visitors. Some leisure seasons are long and some short. Such seasons are a matter of *climate*, regular changes in weather patterns of temperature, rain- and snowfall, sun, and water fluctuations.

Weather is day to day rather than seasonal. Mean temperatures and average rainfall only suggest probabilities, not what it will be like the next week. Forecasts on *weather.gov* are good for a few days ahead, but not far enough in advance for most leisure planning involving travel. So there are inevitable disappointments that may not only spoil an experience but also make a return unlikely. Some recreation businesses offer discounts for a return visit or event, sometimes called a rain check. However, time cannot be banked or compensated. If a rafting trip is marred by rain or a ski week by melting snow, some financial adjustment may be possible. But time cannot be refunded, which is often a more scarce resource than money.

What does this imply for a leisure-based business? To begin, we need to examine climate conditions carefully to minimize weather disappointments. Second, we need to be realistic about the season. When climate is combined with school timetables, 3-day weekends, and other general time factors, what looks like several months of outdoor recreation weather may be reduced to a few weeks. Location is not just place, but it is also time.

Case: Can Climate Be Your Friend?

A viable business was developed on the premise that most sailing in the Great Lakes is in the summer and in the Caribbean in the winter. The business model was to arrange short-term rentals of boats so that owners could put their crafts in the program for times they were not using them and to arrange rentals in the alternative season for owners whose boats were located in one climate or the other. The business operator did not need to own any boats, only to arrange rentals, provide maintenance and storage at a fee, and collect a percentage of the rent. And those rents are not cheap!

Government: Partner or Competition?

Overall, federal government spending on recreation provisions is tiny. A Congressional Budget Office estimate of direct federal spending on recreation was .25 of 1% of the total budget. However, that does not include land management and stewardship. The term *natural-resource-based recreation* usually refers to activity on public land or water. The allocation of resources and management policies and practices are critical for many business plans.

In some cases, government operations compete with the market sector. Federal, state, and sometimes local agencies offer campgrounds, picnic areas, boat launching, ski slopes, and other amenities. In some national parks and recreation areas, government management plans involve leasing facilities to private operators. These leases give the operator a virtual monopoly for on-site lodging, eating, and facility-based activities such as skiing, boating, rafting, and climbing. These leases offer business opportunities, but usually require the business to have a history of successful operation and adequate financial backing. Competing with established franchisees when leases come up for renewal every 10 years or so is possible for some businesses, but not simple.

However, overall the relationship of public sector providers and market sector businesses is symbiotic rather than competitive. Some of the best RB opportunities are located near public sites and provide necessary resources for the activity. Examples are too numerous to list. They involve equipment rental and repair, food, lodging, instruction, transportation, and a wide variety of retail goods and services. Of course, the best initial research for such investment possibilities is on-site and compares a number of locations to identify possible new or improved services. Sometimes an entrepreneurial success in one location can be duplicated in another. Often badly managed businesses can be bought or leased and then improved.

We need to consider several issues:

- Personal enthusiasm for a site or activity is no substitute for rigorous research and evaluation.
- "The best ones are already taken" does not only apply to dating and marriage markets.
- The quality of the public resource is crucial and largely out of the control of the business owner. Plans for future maintenance and development are usually available. Government funding levels, however, may change unpredictably.
- When local cooperation for infrastructure and zoning is required, an assessment of the political climate is basic.
- Symbiosis calls for cooperation, not competition. A good working relationship with public managers is important. But remember that they have to produce numbers and income like a business in competition for funding. Don't expect them to hand over their best revenue streams.
- Cooperative planning is crucial. Sometimes business owners can be members of a formal planning process. On other issues, they can only have input with little influence. But they have to be there!
- Changes in government or management can seriously affect support for particular activities. For example, on a reservoir, new rules on powerboats can degrade fishing or sailing.
- Governments have long-term investments in the resource that involve traditions, if not contracts. However, the more flexibility a business maintains, the less the chance of catastrophic failure. Exit strategies are not a bad idea, even for a new business investment.

The common bias on the part of many voters that every public program and resource should at least break even and even show a profit remains. The fact is that this may lead to overuse and quality deterioration, or it may negatively affect management that is under pressure to produce short-term results at the cost of long-term resource quality. An important strategy is for managers of auxiliary businesses to work with and support public sector managers when they seek to maintain or improve resource quality. After all, that is the basis of supporting businesses.

One implication of this symbiosis or win–win approach to the public–market relationship is that government is not the enemy. Slogans about "big government" or prejudices against the commonly hardworking and underpaid public employees will poison what needs to be a mutually supportive relationship. Of course, there are mistakes and even sloth in any organization (even universities). But my own experience working with U.S. Forest Service and other public personnel is that they are generally capable and care about the stewardship of the resources they manage. At least, that ought to be the attitude in which business interests begin a relationship.

Question

How common is government–market cooperation?

Clue: When is it necessary?

The Always Present Context of Business: Law

There is a great deal of rhetoric about government regulation and the stifling of business enterprise. It is certainly true that any business enterprise operates in a climate of law and regulation. A list of relevant laws might include the following categories:

- the uniform commercial code governing doing business in every state,
- contract law and breach-of-contract law with penalties,
- agency authorizing action on behalf of others,
- tort law regarding injury,
- property law defining ownership, and
- bankruptcy and business dissolution.

For the most part, such law helps provide defined and regular contexts for business. Without such protection, business would be impossible. However, law also involves limitations and some regulations that can be costly. How about this list of regulations?

- Location and operation: zoning; blue laws; fire protection; sign restrictions; fair personnel practices; contracts such as franchises; and real-estate law on leases, mortgages, and property transfer
- Products and services: patents and copyrights, trademarks, Robinson-Patman restrictions of favoritism of large corporations, product safety, liability, warranty and guarantee, mail and phone purchasing, delivery, inventory, and labeling

- Promotion: truth in advertising, truth in credit, bait-and-switch prohibition, Green River Ordinance prohibiting door-to-door sales, and cooling-off law for limited cancellation
- Pricing: unit measure labeling, accurate marking, collusion restrictions for price fixing, sale advertising, fair-trade laws (if enforced)

Debate

In general, do such regulations get in the way of operating a profitable business or provide a level playing field without which business would be impossible? How can we differentiate rules of the game from overregulation?

Back to Time: *Carpe Diem* and All That

"Seize the day" is good advice in relation to an RB in several ways. In terms of investment opportunities, someone else often takes the best chances when another's investors are too slow to come to a decision. Research has demonstrated that alleged experts in stock market investment are unable to time the market and that the good judgment that produces a good yield in one year seldom is repeated the next year. In other words, there is a lot of randomness in the market.

However, in business strategy, some times are better than others. A public agency may implement plans to expand or improve a resource, creating new business opportunities that are unlikely to be available long. The activity life cycle of a new product or activity is only in its initial period of growth for a brief time, and its decline from its peak may come fairly quickly. Getting out ought to be more than a matter of luck.

Innovation and promotion, by the RB or others, may open new opportunities. The problem is that no promotion can produce more than a temporary surge in a business with structural limitations. However, some potential markets can be exploited if the timing is right. As suggested, distinguishing the hot new thing from a promotion-fueled fad requires careful market analysis. On the other hand, those who jumped into handheld electronic game development early are now retiring early and well. Recall that this innovation enhanced what large numbers of people were doing already without requiring radical change in life patterns.

One other way in which *carpe diem* is relevant to investment is in the decision processes of potential clients. In personal leisure decisions, people frequently make snap decisions and jump to an opportunity. As we will analyze further, reaching the System 1 processes of potential markets can be an important marketing approach. "No one has to do it" may quickly switch to "let's do it," especially when there is synergy and support from other people.

More Time Stuff: Timetables and Schedules

As presented, leisure time is generally not leftover time. It is chosen, sometimes in a careful budgeting of the hours of a day or the days of a week or month, and sometimes in a flash of positive emotion. In any case, time allocated to leisure is chosen rather than residual. It tends to be carved out of the endless possibilities and obligations of life. For example, deciding to play with one person may leave significant others behind and even create later obligations.

For many people, there is no spare time. As suggested, leisure time is a choice not a residue. Added to this are a number of social changes that affect how and when leisure choices are made. The big one is the increase of women in the workforce, especially mothers of preschool- and school-aged children. The priorities of child care and nurture as well as play have to be organized around work schedules. School hours tend to be fixed. Work timetables are, for most people, under the control of others who do not organize them for the benefit of employees. However, such women still desire some time for themselves, even if it is limited. The big change, however, is that the assumption that women are generally available for nonwork activity during the day is blown to pieces. This means that the evening and weekend hours formerly reserved for men have to be adjusted for employed women as well. Also, recreation opportunities for children can no longer be scheduled with the assumption that mothers can be around-the-clock chauffeurs and organizers.

Along with the employment of women, there is the shift to 24/7 services. The standard workweek is gone for the 80 to 90% of workers in services. A further complication is that many service employees in retailing, health care, and other operations do not know more than a week in advance when they will be working. So the assumption that people can schedule leisure engagements with a full set of obligations and choices in mind is gone for many adults. Think what this does to the traditional series of events such as instruction in arts, sports, or whatever. The 24/7 timetables threaten every traditional assumption about institutional timetables such as church services, school sports, and public events.

One result of such schedule demands is the increased popularity of the mini-vacation. Three-day weekends or extra days attached to weekends may be reserved for leisure events that require a block of time, but no longer the full week. Such mini-breaks are especially attractive for households with more than one employed adult. Synchronizing a 3-day event may be more feasible than an entire week.

The clear implication is that this threatens all timetables based on the old workweek and traditional business schedules. Even bankers' hours have turned into 24/7 operations in which competition is severe. For those who would resist such a radical change, the realistic response is, "Get over it!"

Some of the problems for an RB are obvious. Regular schedules are problematic and the size of weekly group activities may be reduced. More women's activities will be in the evening and on weekends, which creates space conflicts with what had been men's preserves. Sometimes men will shut women out of some activities as a way of expressing resentment at losing former privilege.

On the other hand, there are also new opportunities. Clever identification of when and where people are working may reveal odd hours for activity. Both women and men may engage in leisure before and after work, during long lunch breaks and on weekends, and in flexible rather than at fixed times. One problem for the business may be the need to employ staff in such odd hours and have buildings open and ready for 18 rather than 8 hours. The result of seeking extended markets can be increased operation costs.

Question

Which changes in social and work timetables inhibit leisure most? Which present opportunities?

Hint: Household composition is still relevant.

Perennial Questions

Two constant questions are dealt with elsewhere. In Chapter 7, we introduced how to tell trends from fads. In Chapter 9, we addressed how participants make leisure decisions and how marketing can address the process.

However, there are two other questions related to time and place. The first is, how far and how long? Analysis of how far potential clients

---

will go for an activity depends on its attractiveness and whether it is a frequent or occasional engagement. Such analysis has to be specific to the activity, location, and type of target market. The question of duration or how much time a client will invest in an activity is specific to the nature of the engagement and the composition of the market. A weekly golf game with a regular group may capture a half day of precious time, whereas a gardening project may be put off for weeks. Conversely, a commitment to children may outweigh all other possibilities and have scheduling priority.

Surprisingly, time and distance may be more important than price to many target markets. Cost may rule out some possibilities from consideration but not be of first importance within the range of engagement considered. Personal and relational priorities and commitments are difficult to assess, but are often most salient to leisure choices. More on this in the next chapter.

Then add to these complications the fact that competition is everywhere. Whether large or small, no market goes unmet for long. So on to decision making.

For reference use:

The Structure of Recreation Research

1. **PARTICIPATION**
   - **By activity**
   - **By "families" of activities (e.g., those related to camping)**
   - **By types of site and resources**
   - **By user groups**
   - **By participation styles**

2. **TRENDS: Measured changes over time in participation categories**

3. **SATISFACTIONS**
   - **Types of satisfactions by activity, resource, social group style, and life course**
   - **Trends in satisfactions and orientations**

4. **OPPORTUNITIES**
   - **Public and private sector resources for activities**
   - **Location of resources and relative access**
   - **Current use of resources**

Research is expensive in time, money, and expertise. Often business decisions are made based on best estimates and educated guesses. But this is no excuse for making System 1 investment choices. Don't let System 2 be lazy!

CHAPTER 9:
MAKING LEISURE DECISIONS

Marketing for a recreation-based business is more than product promotion. Compare the process with selling a car or kitchen appliance. With the car or range, there is necessity. Some purchases are upgrades, but there is usually push as well as pull. Something is unsatisfactory about the current item, from full failure to stylistic dissatisfaction. National advertising supports the promotion. Often underlying the decision will be ratings of quality from consumer organizations. A System 2 decision then considers competition from other dealers and other brands. Although some sales are engineered once the consumer is on the lot or in the store and impulse decisions are not unknown, for the most part the competition, now augmented by all sorts of websites, is fully known to the seller and buyer.

With a leisure purchase, there is no necessity. Remember Rule 1. Generally, there is no national advertising base. Competition is most often a different activity unknown to the seller, or the consumer may choose to do nothing special at all. Decisions, with a lack of evaluative information, often resemble System 1 more than System 2. Most important, recreation businesses are selling an experience, not products that can be at least mentally placed side-by-side and subjected to a cost-benefit analysis. Even a travel package with lots of competition may boil down to an "I've always wanted to see" rather than an online comparison of hotel amenities. In brief, the anticipated experience has to have its own appeal. The big question is how to enhance that appeal.

Which System, or Both?

According to Kahneman (2011), System 1 is largely preanalytical, even impulsive. It consists of a set of prejudgment elements and associations. In a sense, the decision process itself is prerational and emotional. System 2 weighs alternatives, assesses what is known and unknown, and analyzes the process as well as the decision.

It would be tempting for recreation providers to declare all recreation choices as System 1 and then base marketing on evoking positive emotions in relation to the anticipated experience. Then all the marketing that is primarily analytical, comparative, and based on cost–benefit analysis would be ruled out. That would, of course, be hasty and short-sighted. For example, when deciding whether to fly or drive to a vacation destination, most people compare price as well as convenience, recollections of previous good and bad experiences (e.g., at the airport), and time costs. In selecting which golf course to play, players usually figure in price versus crowding on weekends.

Recreation providers need to consider elements of both decision systems in marketing. The system types are, after all, heuristic devices to aid analysis, not either-or real-life descriptions. However, given that, in what follows we tend to emphasize System 1 elements because they tend to be overlooked in most conventional economic models and approaches.

Marketing to System 1

The basic principle, then, is that an RB is selling the experience. There are many secondary or contributing factors such as environment, equipment, learning process, personal relationships, and so on. But basic, especially to promotion, is bringing to the client's attention some associations or recollections of a positive experience. Ideally, the images are of a peak experience that makes costs worthwhile or even causes them to be forgotten.

In Chapters 10 and 13, we go deeper into the elements of leisure experience and what tends to create highs. At this point, we focus on two themes.

The First Factor in Satisfaction: Other People

Different approaches to identifying the elements that contribute most to a good experience almost all come out with the same result: other people. Setting aside for the moment solitary activity, what makes or breaks most experiences is whom we are with. Often those companions are our primary relations from family, household, or other central relationships. Conversely, being with the wrong people can degrade even a rafting trip through the Grand Canyon.

Highest happiness tends to come from doing something we like with the people most important to us. In other situations, engaging new relationships with people we find interesting and attractive can also yield high levels of positive feelings. Some relationships are reliable and comfortable and others new and exciting. However, in general, the people come first. It is usually not difficult for us to recall events in which other people spoiled some activity or place we enjoy.

As a result, marketing is generally most effective when the experience being sold is associated with people we want to be with. Back when it was assumed that travel markets were dominated by the relatively young, there were all the sand, sun, and sex illustrations designed to lure that target market. Now that more mature markets such as postparental adults and the active old are emphasized, the photo strategy becomes a bit trickier. However, other people are still central.

The main implication is clear. Once target markets are identified for whatever the business is selling, advertising and other promotion should highlight the other people that those in the target market most likely to want to be with. It may be couple oriented, same or other sex singles, children who can play with children, or intellectually stimulating oldsters. All of these associations and others are central to selling the experience. As we will stress in Chapter 13, they are also central to management and operation of the business.

System 1 Marketing

The aim of System 1 marketing is to associate the offering with symbols that evoke memories or aspirations of positive experiences. The strategy involves analyzing the primary elements of the experience and selecting symbols—visual, verbal, or combinations—that are likely to prompt positive memories or anticipations. It can be different from a rational cost–benefit analysis. It is likely to involve images more than ideas. With this strategy, we put these associations foremost and cost-benefit calculations in the background.

As we will analyze further, there is more to such associations than feelings of pleasure. Nonetheless, images, symbols, and other recall "hooks" come first. Of course, attractive environments are important, as are suggestions of doing the activity, whether surfing, hiking, or listening to great music. The intention of the promotion is to guide positive associations. Then when the decision process moves on and may include System 2 elements, the halo effect puts them in a positive light. The evoked set of images or emotions will frame the choices.

System 2 Marketing

This emphasis on evoking positive associations does not mean that the traditional System 2 factors are irrelevant. In fact, for repeat business, and crucial to most leisure businesses, they are all part of the total experience.

Of course, price and place are important. Other than the easy part of pricing (i.e., researching the pricing policies of successful similar businesses and any that might be competition), here are a few clues:

- Begin by analyzing the target markets and their likely financial condition. In some areas, a low initial price may be necessary to get clients started.
- In the same way, make no assumptions about household composition. Too many businesses still emphasize family rates rather than dealing with the variety.
- Analyze the participation styles so that pricing can meet variations in regularity, peak hour use, and group composition.

The point is that pricing is one integral element of the total attraction package. It may not make potential clients *want* to do it, but failure to recognize real-life and financial conditions can keep people away.

We have already addressed the place issue. Access to a sited business can make the difference between regular use and occasional patterns that deteriorate into disappearance. The service provided and its scheduling may determine the importance of the location. It is critical to have a strategy that begins with the understanding that for even the 20 to 25% who do an activity regularly, there are always alternatives. Just being the nearest opportunity does not cut it.

We will address other elements in the experience later. The overriding issue is that *every* aspect of the business strategy should be "enabling." Anything that rules out any segment of target markets should be minimized if it cannot be eliminated.

Marketing to Real Decisions

Not to overstress business school omissions, but there are two sources of inadequacy: the assumption of rational or reasoned choices and a lack of understanding of the special qualities of a recreation-based business. To be fair (somewhat), the reasoned choice models can become successful in prediction. They are, of course, probabilistic. That is, they predict likelihood of certain outcomes given a set of preconditions. For marketing purposes, there are two problems. First, they do not predict for any individual, only for probability within a given set. Second, when devising a marketing strategy, businesses seldom know that much about prospective clients. One reasoned choice model (developed by two colleagues) presupposes the business knowing so much that the model becomes generally unusable.

Here we give attention to the decision process. Again, different models seem more useful. The first considers prerational responses rather than systematic definitions of the situation. Association and emotional halos often count for more in leisure decisions than weighing outcomes, alternatives, and costs. According to Kahneman's (2011) prospect theory, there are other elements in the decision process. A highly significant element is risk aversion. Decisions seem to give greater weight to avoiding loss than reaching goals. For recreation, this suggests that promotions that call up possible threats may turn away clients even when a rational assessment would suggest that the likely outcomes are worth the risk. For example, fear of failing to find acceptance in a group of strangers may keep clients away. It also suggests that the comfort level of a possible experience—in social acceptance, skills required, or evaluative observation by others—may rule out the activity itself.

The trick seems to be for us to associate the contemplated experience with positive symbols and use promotion that does not unintentionally elicit common threats. For example, in sports or the arts, using "stars" to illustrate the activity may turn away the risk averse. I have had a running argument with sports gerontologists who persist in telling about the exceptional swimmers or runners who are world class at age 85 rather than more ordinary folk who stay active with attainable levels of performance. It is known that familiarity reduces the perceived threat of almost anything. (I have flown professional smoke jumpers who were as apprehensive about my routine off-airport landings as I am about jumping out of an airplane.) As we will elaborate further, in marketing recreation businesses want to associate the experience value of what they are selling with what minimizes social or competence threats.

> **Question**
>
> Describe a picture of high moments of your favorite activity. How might this high suggest a marketing strategy?
>
> **Hint:** The content may be more than emotional.

Implications for Promotion and Marketing

This is not a program. Recreation businesses are too varied for that. But some hints and clues can be useful. The first is to identify the peak experiences related to the activity and setting. We can do this by asking current participants what they remember as most enjoyable from previous events. There is also some pointed research on the subject (Chapters 13 and 14). It is the peaks that tend to draw clients back and the valleys that turn them off.

The two foci are simply what people do and whom they are with. The action component may be multifaceted. However, the core is the part of the total experience in which players are most fully engaged.

The community/intimacy factor may vary for even the same client. Although most of those in consistent primary relationships—family, lovers, close friend—find the highest satisfaction over time in those ties, there may be singular events in which some element of novelty becomes salient. For example, bars and clubs in which the "fancy milling" is designed to explore new relationships may feature novelty. The same theme may seem rather unexciting, but it is still important for older adults who have lost primary companions. Sorry if this is belaboring the other people theme, but it is too often neglected in business schemes and management.

The competence theme is important to people of all ages. Opportunities to demonstrate ability are central to many recreation experiences. It may be surprising that this element of satisfaction does not seem to lessen with age. It is obvious for the striving and developing youth. However, perhaps because of questions raised by aging, it is also central for older adults as they seek to maintain and even strengthen their sense of competent selfhood.

There are other clues related to System 1 marketing. One is familiarity. Just the opposite of challenge, returning to places and people that have produced good experiences in the past is also a recurrent motif. Most people do not want to be challenged or seeking novelty all the time. However, in marketing, this element may need relatively little attention.

A kind of bipolar framework underlies some recreation marketing. One end includes the experiential highs of engagement and relationships. The other end includes inertia. Inertia is the extreme of the no-one-has-to-do-it factor. For RB marketing, inertia in all its forms is the enemy. If we include the now omnipresent home and portable games and entertainment within the inertia spectrum, then inertia may be the big foe.

How can this inertia be overcome in marketing? We examine the nature of leisure experiences further to begin to find answers.

Application

To what extent will your anticipated business (real or imagined) be social? Try to list positive social elements in one column and negative in another. How do they balance out? How can good management enhance the positive and eliminate the negative?

Discussion

If in a group (class) environment, choose an activity in which all or most have engaged recently and list all the factors that would make them *not* want to return. Are most of these factors social or based in the nature of the activity?

Question

When you choose a recreation-based destination resort, is recreation the icing on the cake or the primary consideration? If the latter, are many resort and hotel websites and ads misdirected? Check some out.

Case: If you believe that accommodations come first, look at the Club Med promotions and advertising. What comes first? Activity or social groups? Or both? What's the icing now?

One other dimension: resort differentiation by central activity. Try that one out in your tourism and hospitality class.

CHAPTER 10:
WHAT DOESN'T CHANGE ... MUCH

When one has been doing and interpreting research in a field for over 40 years, there is the danger of becoming embedded in old models and approaches. Being a scientist, including a social scientist, means to never stop learning, because current knowledge is always partial and subject to revision. Some of the perspectives employed in this book are quite recent; others are quite old. In this book, the premise is that the age of a model or theme neither validates nor invalidates it. Also, the latest thing may be just another fad.

In this chapter, we begin with some explanatory approaches that have been around for some time, even decades. That does not make them eternal truths to be worshiped as iconic and immutable. Nor does it make them outmoded and useless. In fact, some are extremely valuable in assessing markets and strategies for recreation businesses.

Social Contexts

Sartre did a disturbing play in which the theme was that "hell is other people." (Are there any people with whom you would want to be enclosed in a room forever?) In any given context, that may be true in this life as well. A small group tour in a van or yacht accompanied by two or three unpleasant people can be a disaster. However, most often, people seek leisure settings and activities where they will be with people they value and enjoy. In fact, in urban areas (where most people live), people are more likely to make friends in recreation engagement than work, especially if that includes children's play programs and religious, sports, and arts organizations.

Kahneman (2011, p. 395) reports one of countless studies that found that given reasonable health and a measure of economic security, the major factor in life satisfaction is regular interaction with people we enjoy and care for. That primary group may change as we move through the life course, but having contact with friends and loved ones remains central to a "good day." This is repetition here, but it is so important that it needs to be repeated as a premise for any analysis that follows.

The Life Course and Predictable Changes

Social psychologists tend to use the term *life span*, but that label overemphasizes chronological age. Family sociologists used to refer to the *family life cycle*, but that makes it seem too regular and predictable. *Life course* suggests that there is a progression related to common transitions, but that each journey is unique and subject to unpredictable changes. (For a fuller account of this approach in relation to recreation, see Kelly's, 2012, *Leisure* or earlier editions of the same.)

The point is that there are sequences of changes in social contexts up to the end of any life journey. These changes, whether sudden or predictable transitions, affect leisure interests, companions, resources, and orientations. First, however, a warning: Few people make the normative journey all the way without disruptions. More choose or are forced into variations. For example, over half of the children in this country will experience some period without a pair of parents in their home, and, so evident at this time, the predictable work "career" has become a series of jobs for most adults.

Beginning with school years, the traditional life course goes something like this:

- Preparation: education and other getting-ready settings
  * Seeking to establish a new household
  * Entering the world of work, hopefully one with a future
- Establishment:
  * Early: seeking regularity in primary relationships and work
  * Middle: consolidating home and work including marriage and children for most
  * Late: launching children (hopefully) and settling for a position in a work trajectory
- Consolidation and Acceptance:
  * Preretirement and accepting who and where one is
  * Retirement and aging: reestablishment without work structure
  * Reinvestment despite limited future
  * Frailty and death

This roughly is the predictable pattern. Some of the transitions greatly affect leisure meanings, contexts, and resources. Leaving school and the parental household are obvious. Becoming a parent seems to cause greater change than marriage itself. Late midlife with its recognition that the end is nearer than the beginning and prospects are limited can turn work limits into recreation investments. Retirement, of course, transforms timetables and obligations as well as income for most. Frailty, at an age no one can predict, closes off many leisure experiences.

Then there are the traumatic events. Divorce or death end what is for most the primary relationship and may come at any age. Loss of employment affects every aspect of life, especially economic security. One study I directed in Peoria, Illinois, examined transitions in the life course, focusing on age 40 and older (Kelly, 1987). Not surprisingly, most individuals had at least one major and unpredictable life-changing event, and most had found resources within themselves or with others to come through the trauma and rebuild life. Further, for those coping with change, leisure investments were an important positive factor.

Three important perspectives are relevant here for recreation marketing and management:

1. Identifying where your clients are in the life course gives critical information about their goals, obligations, schedules, resources, and associations. For example, cultivating a daytime market of preschool parents has usually meant offering some means of child care. Now, however, those parents are usually in the workforce, so time is the scarce factor and flexibility crucial. On the other hand, retirees have flexibility but often seek social contexts to replace work. To be realistic, some life course periods pretty much rule out recreation that is costly in time as well as finances.

2. The big change is that a predictable life course with regular periods and passages is now a minority pattern. Further, leisure engagements may serve to aid transitions and especially offer social contexts for those who have to rebuild. The explosion of online matching services suggests that some recreation programs may be missing a vital opportunity, one that is more than singles bars and love cruises. It is in the ordinary round of life that people are most likely to meet and engage enjoyable and compatible others. With all the problems of work relationships, that leaves leisure.

3. A gradual shift in sexual norms has already had impacts, with many of the implications yet to be understood. A generation, and certainly two, ago, seeking sexual access led many into marriage. Now sexual access is more widely available and accepted as a new norm by large segments of the population. The changes include both genders, all education levels, differing sexual identities, most ethnic identifications, and ages flirting with legal limits. Further, with numbers skewed toward lower education levels,

about half of all babies are born to unmarried mothers. Consider what this does to the former family life cycle with predictable periods and transitions. Also, think about how the greater openness to intimate sexual activity, a trend that began over a century ago, has transformed the expectations and behaviors in and around many recreation settings. The way a business responds to such changes will have to be worked out in the local situation; perhaps the urban scene needs to be differentiated from the family-oriented suburb. In any case, the frequency with which meeting leads to something more transforms the sexual dimensions of many recreation settings.

Case

A fitness center transformed from a former racquet club in a fast growing high-tech development did an analysis of its market segments. Easy to identify were younger males really into body development, younger professional women combining meeting peers with fitness, older women seeking to maintain body shape and condition, younger males and females for which the center was a meeting place, and a scattering of clients just seeking access to the equipment. The key to dealing with diversity was differential scheduling and marketing. Without going into details, it was discovered that the early morning before-work exercisers tended to be young males. After-work time was crowded. Evening attracted socially oriented younger women and men. The middle-aged women preferred gender segregation.

Map out a timetable. What about weekends? How are they different? Then how would you design advertising and promotions? (Whoever said all of this was easy?)

The new majority is people in transition. Jobs, families, locales, and values change. People learn and hopefully grow through the life journey. As work seems more and more limited for most adults and traditional institutions lose appeal, then there we have it: the multipurpose recreation business (RB).

One constant element of leisure is change. That is, there seems an almost inevitable mixture of commitment to activities that people find especially satisfying and those they like to explore. Both are significant, as the life journey is characterized by change as well as predictability. The challenge of something new is contrasted with the comfort of something familiar. In terms of numbers, the market for familiarity is probably the greater. The central market for an activity opportunity is usually those who would like to do it more or in an improved setting.

Targeting markets may begin with the population and participation numbers, but it does not end there. There is more than one path to recreation engagement, from doing something familiar with friends to taking the risk of something new with strangers. Marketing can address both, but not necessarily in the same style or medium. Management can be sensitive to the needs of both, if not necessarily simultaneously. (I cannot count the number of tennis facilities that do not seem to respond to visitors who do not know anyone and are not there for a 7-day clinic. For example, my center has offered a simple sign-up schedule that welcomes visitors and does not require elaborate arrangements through staff.)

Other Limits: Economic and Cultural

In terms of market assessment, there is a seeming dilemma. For at least two decades, the purchasing power of most of the population has declined. Those with substantial investments have ample discretionary income. Those highly educated or skilled also have discretionary income for leisure, but often are under heavy time pressures. The middle mass who are employed have on average diminished income to spend on recreation. Then the 40% of the poor or near poor are, of course, restricted in nonessential spending.

The dilemma is this: Recreation provisions for the upper 5 to 15% are most likely to be priced for an adequate profit. This is hardly a secret. Therefore, market sector provisions are heavily skewed toward that market sector. The result? Competition. The favored target market for any provision that is costly is, of course, those with discretionary income and preferably lots of it.

On the other hand, in many locations, the middle mass, the 45 to 60%, are underserved. A business plan that can reach that market and still make a profit may beat the failure odds. But how? The provider can piggyback on public facilities and environments to minimize investment and maximize the potential market, or the provider can offer services such as summer wilderness hiking, water sport instruction, reasonable rental opportunities, and hunting and fishing guiding rather than facilities. These are just two of many strategies.

Clues to such strategies? Location, experience with the activity base, flexibility, part-time employees such as students, and a host of other ways of limiting initial investment and operating costs.

Research

Try a walk-around observation at a public recreation site. Who is there? What are they doing?

Hint: Most people at the beach are not swimming.

What potential markets does this observation suggest?

There are also cultural limits on what clients are willing to attempt and to pay for. For example, Hispanic families seem less likely to divide up for leisure than Anglo units. In some cultures, there remain different definitions of what is appropriate for young women than for young men. Sports take a higher place than the arts in some cultures. Styles of music that attract some groups repel others.

There are cultural changes. However, we are not "plastic personalities" who can readily adjust to almost any situation. Many of the persistent cultural themes are related to gender. Others pertain to what people wear, the composition of vocabularies, and specific contextual behaviors. One clue to sensitive understanding of cultural elements in a RB is to get out from behind the desk and closely observe what is going on. Ms. or Mr. Entrepreneur, everyone is not just like you.

Everything Does Not Work

There is no substitute for constant and systematic evaluation. A business school will, quite appropriately, demonstrate how good accounting practices can be central to monitoring a business and identifying what is not working. A spreadsheet that allocates income and expenditures by the various sectors of a business and even by market sectors can identify many errors in operation and what might best be expanded.

However, again, there is no substitute for getting out there and observing. Numbers are relatively easy. Mapping spatial use and adding up time uses need not require a computer. Analysis will often identify space that is not being used and space that is crowded, time spent in conversation in and around an activity rather than in direct play, groupings who do or do not participate together, and secondary activity that is part of the experience but does not require dedicated and designed space. Traffic patterns are important. Gathering points, often not designed for socializing at all, may lead to more efficient design and enjoyable experiences.

But the manager has to be willing to be wrong! If concepts, designs, and operational styles are to be defended rather than evaluated, then the business is headed for trouble. New clients, who are highly desired, may bring with them different styles of play and socializing.

What Is *the* Leisure Experience . . . If Any?

Various scholars and self-ordained philosophers have written about *the* leisure experience. The mere fact that they do not all designate the same experience suggests the topic may be more complicated. Contemporary designs intended to produce positive outcomes are more complex than those focused on a single theme. For example, the constantly changing and developing epitome of RB, Walt Disney World, has excitement and relaxation, challenge and comfort, high technology and simple themes, education and entertainment. There seems to be an infinite variety of things for sale, many themed to match the exhibits and rides. Shows, rides, 3-D multiscreens, surround sound, and so on are aimed at a range of ages and groupings. If any elements are consistent, they are high quality and cost. (Also, note the change in response to market research. In Orlando, the much touted Epcot [Experimental Prototype Community of Tomorrow] showcasing new technologies changed from a proposed real community, to a showcase of exhibits, and now, admitting problems, to another development).

The point is that leisure experience is embedded in the activity and the environment. The core experiences of the arts vary for performance and appreciation. Engagement in competitive sport is certainly different from being a spectator. White-water kayaking and beach sunning both involve water, but in different ways.

Further, experiences are multidimensional. Is there, for example, a "wilderness experience"? Those who read the literature of various conservation organizations might believe in such a global concept. Counter to this, a social psychologist, B. L. Driver, doing research for the U.S. Forest Service explored reported backcountry experiences and found a rather complex scheme. My summary of the results (Kelly, 2012, p. 290) includes the following schema:

- **Social:** social recognition, family togetherness, being with friends, meeting new people, exercising leadership, and sharing skills
- **Personal expression and development:** achievement, reinforcing self-image, competition/testing, discovering and learning in reflection and physical fitness
- **Experimental (intrinsic):** stimulation, risk taking, tranquility, using equipment, and nostalgia
- **Nature appreciation:** enjoyment of scenery, closeness to nature, learning, open space, and privacy
- **Change:** rest, escape from pressure and routines, avoiding crowds, and getting away from problems

Note not only the variety but also the seeming contradictions. And this in only one type of recreation environment and related set of activities. It does not represent basketball, distance running, painting, dancing, or a hundred other activities. How is it possible to design and program for such variety?

NSP and Recreation Marketing

In my 1985 *Recreation Business* book, I offer a provisional outline of the variety of leisure needs that may be satisfied by different types of activity. The NSP (Need Satisfaction Potential) scheme has never been measured, but does suggest themes that may be employed in marketing and design of an RB:

The following represents only a fraction of the types of leisure needs or satisfaction:

- Rest, relaxation, work contrast
- Skill development and mastery
- Self-expression
- Personal growth
- Excitement and contest
- Exercise and health
- Companionship and belonging

Note that the NSPs are not mutually exclusive. Rather, a particular activity or environment can yield multiple satisfactions. The point here is that identification of such satisfactions can guide advertising and operational principles.

> **Question**
>
> Connect your favorite activity or RB project with these or other possible outcomes. Is this a possible planning approach?

First, personal experience with the activity base of an RB is essential. Along with personal experience, listening to and observing others in the same environment will add to your analysis. With a clue from Driver's results, recognize that everyone in a recreation environment or activity may not gain the same outcomes and satisfactions. For example, a retiree at the tennis center may seek challenge and involvement, whereas a stressed employed mother may hope for separation and relaxation. Both may be experienced in the same setting and in different styles of engagement in the same activity. To add to the complexity, think about the multiple experience dimensions of travel; a nightclub with drinking, eating, dancing, and entertainment; or a workshop in ceramics design.

Second, one way to sort out the experiences requires identifying peak experiences in an activity or involvement sequence. What are the elements that are, if not unique, at least special to an activity and setting? Are the peak experiences the same for every participant in a particular event or activity? However, it is most often the peaks that draw a client back to the business, and peaks are especially crucial to marketing and management if target markets are to be attracted and nurtured.

Peak Experiences: Flow and Skill

Two lines of research point to central dimensions of peak experiences. Significantly, it is those who experience such highs who are most likely to be regular participants, invest time and money, and become the core of the market spectrum for any particular activity or setting.

Flow: The Meeting of Skill and Challenge

Mihaly Csikszentmihalyi (1976) is an innovative research psychologist whose adoption of the concept of flow has received wide attention in a variety of quarters. The basis is simple: People in flow experience a condition in which they become so absorbed in an activity that they lose consciousness of time and place and of anything other than deep involvement in the action. This state occurs when there is a meeting of challenge and of skill or competence. When skill is greater than the challenge, the result is boredom. When the challenge is too great for the skill, the result is anxiety. Satisfaction, then, results in some middle range of a viable skill–challenge situation.

His research approach has been based on experience sampling, in which at a random time, an attention-getting signal calls a person to pause and record what she or he is doing, where, with whom, mood, and level of satisfaction and involvement. Across all age ranges and in a variety of activities, flow, satisfaction, and positive mood are highest in that skill–challenge concurrence. Obvious settings for identifying flow include sports, creative arts, learning difficult skills, and others involving recreation activities. He and his colleagues also confirm the general finding that involvement in communication with valued associates including intimacy may produce a similar high. (I suggest an extension of the concept to the correlate of social flow.)

Implications for an RB are self-evident. Any design or management that can increase the likelihood of skill–challenge involvement is most likely to produce experiences that will create return business and that most effective advertising, word of mouth. How flow can be supported and enhanced in any setting depends on a number of social and environmental factors, which vary with the activity. However, the peaks of flow may be the most consistent experiences in attractive leisure offerings.

Amateurs: The Dedicated Core

Robert Stebbins (1979) developed the concept of amateurs out of his own experience as a nonprofessional chamber music player. He has since investigated a wide range of activities: magic, baseball, archaeology, theater, and others. His findings are a correlate to Csikszentmihalyi's. The amateur does not depend on the activity for his or her primary income. It is, however, central to the amateur's personal and social identity, investment of time and money, primary relationships, and life satisfaction. In some cases, as with musicians and (in the old days) baseball players, there may be some pay per performance to create semipros. In the arts of painting, ceramics, writing, and others, those most adept may insist on selling their creations as a validation, even though the income may not be central to household finances. As with flow, the skill and challenge are central. Further, according to Stebbins, the standards of performance for amateurs are much the same as those for professionals.

Such amateurs can be the core of a stable market for many businesses. Further, their performances may attract others to the activity. In some situations, they may be part-time instructors in required skills. Additionally, their enthusiasm for the activity, especially when it is immediate in contrast to televised professionals, may be a major form of unpaid promotion for a business.

The central dimensions in flow and for amateurs are constant skills development, challenging settings and materials, regular association with other amateurs seeking flow, and access to opportunities that are feasible and affordable.

Question

How can you apply these two themes to your RB plan or hope? In what ways can you help clients move from entry skills to the deeper satisfactions of skill and challenge?

Clue: Both flow and amateurism involve skill development and other people.

An Often Overlooked Question:
What Do People Actually Do?

Don't we know what people are doing at their kid's ball game, on the beach, while hiking, and so on? A few studies have offered some surprises and raised some interesting issues for a recreation-based business. In trying to answer this question, we can challenge clichés that may mislead the leisure entrepreneur.

To begin, there is golf. A common assumption is that the particular challenges of the sport and the attractions of the outdoor environment compose the activity called golf. However, take a walk around the course and clubhouse to see what else is going on: conversations, arguments, eating and drinking, waiting, keeping score, and a variety of emotional expressions. Over the hours in an event called golf, there is a lot going on, some enjoyable and some not. There are reasons why golf has been called a good walk spoiled. However, that misses the peaks of flow and the satisfactions of skill demonstration and improvement as well as companionship with established groups.

An observational study at Corps of Engineers reservoir beaches in the Pacific Northwest came up with the surprising finding that swimming, boating, and beach sports occupied far less than half the time. Rather, most people most of the time were talking, resting, reading, drinking, flirting, exhibiting themselves in various ways, and staying out of the water (unpublished report, 1976).

What do people do when they are at a tourism destination? Of course, the variety of activity is great. However, for many tourists, the most time-consuming activities are shopping, eating and drinking, and resting. And, of course, there is always picture taking, even strangely, of oneself.

What is the most common away-from-home leisure locale for Americans and many others? It has been clearly the shopping center, especially when the satisfaction of doing something can be gained by purchasing stuff. Things, often inexpensive, are symbols of efficacy for many, without any serious demands on skill. It is not just teens who hang out in the mall. Various attempts to incorporate recreation opportunities within the mega-mall have been met with mixed results. These activities have the advantage of being where people are. How to cope consistently with the crowds, parking, and other barriers has proven problematic. Also, the wide mix of patrons in a mall has limited some activities.

Finally, where does fantasy fit in? The leisure of the mind and imagination, often melding into dreaming, is common for almost everyone. Students of the mind have demonstrated that imaginative activity has many developmental and therapeutic values. For many, the fantasy is connected to real activity. (As a teen ball player, I used to pitch entire White Sox games in my semi-wakeful fantasy mind.) To my knowledge, no one has done convincing research connecting fantasy to leisure choices and satisfactions, but I am sure that the relationship is there. It may even lead to decisions, activity, and time and money investments.

Leisure Investment Issues

The overall theme of this chapter has been relative consistencies in leisure behavior, motivations, satisfactions, and choices. This theme has been related to marketing in some examples and questions. The first issue revolves around central and consistent satisfactions. Other people, skill development and challenge, communities formed around commitment to a common activity, self-identification based on a skilled activity, and peaks such as flow are and are likely to remain central to a recreation experience that people find attractive and want to repeat.

The second consistent theme has more to do with resources, conflicts, and regular associations. The life course is one useful approach for market analysis and targeting. The greater and greater number of deviations from that model and the increasing number of market segments in transition at any time in life's journey also offer attractive marketing opportunities.

It is possible that we can argue that the needs for close and consistent relationships, for gaining and demonstrating competence, and for satisfying self-definitions are found more often in leisure than in work in contemporary society. In any case, recreation is not peripheral, leftover, or trivial to a large number of people, and they are the consistent markets.

There is a wide variety of RB opportunities. Some are large and some small. Even though most entrepreneurs do not begin by envisioning big business, that dimension is a part of the scene that all RB entrepreneurs must consider for their business concept.

Project

!

Your Big Project

If you are in the process of developing a plan for your business, try to demonstrate how the research on the life course, flow, amateurs, and ethnicity may influence the identification and development of target markets?

Your Little Project

What about niche markets? There might be innovations. What do you think of the idea based on observation. Been to a NFL or intercollegiate football game recently? Half or more of the time is time-outs. So what do people do to alleviate boredom? Some look for music, dancing, or other on-field activity. At least as many are playing on their smartphone. What are the pros and cons of establishing a fee-based program purchased at the gate that would offer further entertainment, analysis, and information through the smartphone? Or in what ways would it, like TV, be better free with interspersed commercials?

The point here is not to boost this particular concept, but to illustrate how critical observation might identify a new and different business opportunity. We can revise Kahneman's formula to be, what you see may *not* be all there is if you look again.

CHAPTER 11:
THE BIG PICTURE

Most businesses start out small. However, the recreation business (RB) environment includes some *very big* businesses. They are different in many ways from small start-up operations. However, they are relevant in at least three ways:

- They are a part of the experience economy.
- They may provide business training for those new to the field. (However, for the most part they train people for their own business and pay low hourly rates.)
- Perhaps surprisingly, they may be competition for small experience businesses.

What Is the Experience Economy?

To begin, some leisure-based businesses are really big. Examples include the Disney enterprise, Las Vegas, Netflix, Nike, hotel chains, and restaurant franchises. Size does not always mean quality. However, such businesses have had opportunities to try out different styles, promotions, management approaches, and personnel. They can afford a few mistakes because their size can absorb occasional losses. Usually, they have access to capital, either from their own income or through established credit arrangements.

Anyone in the field can learn from them. However, this does not mean that they do everything right. Big organizations often become resistant to change. As turning a big ship takes time and space, so real shifts for a big corporation meet resistance, usually from those who have seen success in the past from what they have developed. In fact, as a fun activity, we can visit Disney World, a theme park, or a mega-resort with a critical eye to look for practices that seem to block or erode experiences.

Research

If you have access to a major recreation development, arrange a visit. Take notes and write a critique and make recommendations as though you were a $2,000-a-day consultant. (My own experience with such a contract was that such a report was received and filed in a dark place.)

On the other hand, many businesses are sensitive to threats. For example, some theme parks, including Disney, have heard critics deride their "fakery"; these theme parks now seek to design and promote authenticity. Contradictions of designing and producing authenticity seem to present some difficulties. Nonetheless, a fake English pub at Disney World avoids the problems of fighting one's way to the bar for a pint and of getting to the real thing. (Does tapping Guinness make WDW Village an authentic pub? Why or why not?)

It is central, however, that bigness does not preclude the issue of personal experience. An architect may design an office building to make an exterior statement, even at the cost of interior efficiency. The designers of a recreation-based site should keep the hoped-for experience of clients central. We could possibly argue that part of the genius of the WED designers in California was originally this priority. Certainly Walt himself set out with the family experience in mind when he took the great leap from animated films to the pioneer Disneyland.

One Approach: Business as Theater

The metaphor of business as theater is borrowed from a book by Joseph Pine and James Gilmore (1999). They argue that more and more businesses are marketing an experience rather than a fixed product. Further, the experience is largely leisure based. However, such experience is more than entertainment. It involves eliciting a response from the clients who become involved in the total experience.

Without getting too deeply into the "dramaturgical" background of this approach, we know that the theater metaphor is very suggestive. It suggests that an RB does more than provide a service. Rather, the outcome involves reciprocity between the provider and the client. Even big leisure businesses focus on the individual and small-group experience. Big markets call for customization more than a mass phenomenon. (You might do a critique of much of the Las Vegas style from this standpoint.) In fact, the aim becomes experience that involves the client. Pine and Gilmore call this transformation.

That is, something occurs in the encounter between the provision and the participant. Although their examples of fitness and religion seem a bit weak, the idea that something happens to the participant is on target. The experience may be intense and involving (flow), or it may be more diffuse as a form of entertainment. In any case, as in theater, in an RB there is reciprocity between the stage and the audience. And good theater is designed to produce that involvement, not just put on a play.

Again, the aim of an RB is the experience, usually a process with highs and lows. The business offers an environment, a setting, a design, a process, or a "play" that draws the clients into the experience. This is a central theme of this book, as well as of Pine and Gilmore's (1999) offering.

Questions can be raised about the metaphor. Can experience be a product? Is a properly designed environment enough? What is required in terms of preparation, personal facilitation, social organization, and symbolic introduction? Consider the tourism dilemma. In general, tourists seem to seek a new experience in a familiar and protected presentation. They may find it difficult to combine novelty and safety in a tour or destination, especially when much of the environment is out of their control. Most travelers seek the challenge of new experiences with a minimum of risk. The extent to which a recreation experience can be designed and predetermined is tested in big business developments such as Las Vegas.

However, one element of the theater metaphor is beyond question. As in the theater, the leisure business environment is designed and operated to maximize positive and involving experiences. One advantage that big businesses enjoy is that, again with Disney World as the epitome, they can control all or most of the environment and change what is not working.

Question

In the business you are considering, are significant elements of the total process out of your control? If so, how can you mitigate possible negative results?

Hint: What elements control the client more? If so, how can you facilitate this?

Follow-up: How much of the experience should be left open? Can good design maximize the experience by fostering involvement and minimizing the show?

Disney Was Right!

Not about everything, but about the target market for a leisure business. The target market is generally the small group, and not only the family as Walt originally envisioned, but also the variety of groups suggested in Chapter 10. It is a small world after all—not in culture as the song suggests, but in where people live most of their lives. The attention of most people most of the time is no more than a few people away. People may care about a wider circle, but they tend to live in small social worlds.

The implications for an RB involve not only marketing but also management and design. If people want to be alone, they generally do not need a business. There is the walk, the park, the library, the theater, and the residence. The RB is most often oriented to a small group, either brought to the site or created on-site in the activity process.

In those small worlds, no two lives are alike. Stuff happens. There is divorce, illness, death, children and spouses with special health needs, accidents, layoffs, business-required moves, and all of the contingencies that disrupt life. All of the schemes for identifying and categorizing people into market segments ignore these realities of life.

It is not heartless to think of how recreation investments, associations, timetables, skills, and anything that helps people rebuild may become crucial to clients. Rather, when work, family, or other associations central to the small worlds are disrupted, recreation may become central to the process of healing. It may not be realistic to see those in such forced transitions as a target market, but being sensitive to the presence and needs of such people is not only about good business practice, but also about making a business more than a place to play.

Especially for older clients, one aspect of this awareness recognizes those who have been involved in an activity, had a health trauma, and are on the road back to full functioning. Often friends and family provide needed support in the recovery process, but often the people involved in the activity are unable to function in a skill-based environment. Sports devotees often do not want to abandon their sport after a heart attack, but need help in getting back into it. It may not qualify as a market, but helping those in the recovery process participate once again in an activity can be a real RB function.

Question

In an RB with which you are familiar, what programs or adaptations might maximize ways to welcome and integrate into the program those who have dropped out of an activity or who are new to the RB?

Reminder: This process may be central to expanding a clientele.

But for the Small Business, It May Be a Big World

On the other hand, many small businesses do not live in an isolated world protected from the big guys. There are many examples.

The first for small businesses is the "big box." In sports, camping, apparel, and other recreation-activity-related items, the big store down the road may sell the same product as a small business, and at "lowest prices always." In many cases, the manufacturers and distributors collaborate in this competition by making low-cost racquets, clubs, tents, and other items for the big boxers. When a Wilson, Prince, or Head tennis racquet is $24 at Walmart and one that looks the same is $175 at the pro shop, why would a beginner not go for price? Golf clubs, balls, bags, shoes, jackets, and other items are there, too. An experienced player may know the difference, but many do not. The RB can concede the low-end market to the big boxes, but that is a great loss of market share.

Second, for most leisure items there are the online suppliers, the "small box." Tennis and golf pro shops, bookstores, and sports clothing retailers, for example, have had to swallow their annoyance at seeing their regulars walk in with new equipment purchased from the national online suppliers. The onliners can offer a complete line of manufacturers, brands, and models. They can have discounts, sales, and clearances that no small local retailer can approach. For the on-site business, it is frustrating when customers browse and try out items and then buy them elsewhere. Right or wrong, it is a fact of retailing in almost any business except those that offer on-site services. The world of retailing has now gone global online with the aid of the worldwide efficient delivery services and their incredible computerized logistics. For any sports equipment, leisure apparel, outdoor gear, instructional literature and visuals, or anything that can be showcased online and delivered in a truck, the competition is from a Big World of business.

Many kinds of recreation businesses require large outlays of capital. Destination resorts, manufacturing of machine-tooled equipment, national or global advertising and distribution, travel packages that involve river and ocean cruising, or anything large scale requires big-time capital. Financing becomes a matter of packaging loans, collateral, professional design and management, and so on, up in the nine-figure stratospheres. The good news is that such operations provide lots of jobs. The bad news is that most entry-level opportunities are, for the most part, low wage, insecure, often seasonal, and dead end *unless* a person has a scarce skill or experience. Some even require the worker to be relatively young and attractive.

Of course, some big businesses create opportunities for auxiliary businesses. The major resort may contract out various services or rent space for small businesses. The problem is that they usually hold on to the major profit centers. On the other hand, rented space reduces capital outlays and consequent risk. It can be an opportunity.

Question

Consider a major beach resort as the environment. Developers plan to open opportunities for rental space for shops and services. The usual beachwear and snack shops are a given. What opportunities for rental and retail businesses might *not* duplicate what everyone else is doing and meet an underserved market?

Hint 1: Try observing or imagining what visitors actually do at the beach?

Hint 2: In what social groups do most beach visitors arrive?

In the Big World,
Is Big Business Where the Opportunities Are?

For some areas, the answer is clearly yes. Capital requirements alone make this a fact. Securing major capital investment from banks, venture capital, and investment trusts calls for more than a good idea and enthusiasm. Some space and equipment can be leased. Some franchises come with capital sources. Some investments can be bought at 30 cents on the dollar following first-generation failure. (This works only when a viable business fails due to undercapitalization.) But the big ones are out there and not likely to go away.

Question

In what kinds of big recreation businesses might someone entering the field have valuable learning experiences?

On the other hand (this again), big businesses have their own problems. Probably the main one is overinvestment in the status quo. It can be nearly impossible for an established leadership team to be receptive to a there-may-be-a-better-way-of-doing-this approach. I can cite as examples my own experience with corporations such as General Motors (in their former set-in-stone management days) or Yamaha (when lack of flexibility cost them millions). For the most part, corporate leaders do not want a new perspective. They tend to rehire consultants who tell them want they want to hear. They keep bright young thinkers on the periphery of decisions. At the same time, they choke out competition. Exceptions? Sure, but do not wait around too long.

Is there a place on the RB spectrum for innovation? Absolutely. But do not expect it to be easy, even when you have facts and figures to support your argument. Kahneman (2011) cites being risk averse as only the beginning of a person or business becoming unable to see how things might be different . . . and better. As a result, those trying to implement some of the ideas from this book are likely to be dismissed, if heard at all.

In such situations, the issue is corporate culture. If you stumble on a corporation in which innovation and self-criticism are the norm, call yourself blessed and apply for a job. However, you may not want to be self-supporting until you find one.

Question

What are some successful innovations in the RB field?

Clue: Cast a wide net, oceans away and down the road.

What Do "Experts" Know?

In any field of business, there are those who sell their expertise. In some cases, they have a financial interest in what they are promoting. The obvious examples are the trade associations that exist by promoting their activity or product. In a recession with grounded forecasts negative, they usually project that next year will see the "beginning of a recovery" every year until eventually they are right.

Those with the latest "great new idea" are often more persuasive. Of course, some of them are right—the idea really is great. Others have one foot in the air and the other on a slippery soapbox. As suggested, the best way to critique the dreamers is with the baseline numbers and trends and with a bunch of hard questions. If the enthusiast eventually blows you off with something like, "You just don't get it," you can just agree. Hard questions ought to be the entrepreneur's bread and butter.

What About New Products?

To begin, we cannot always easily differentiate innovation from promotion. A few hints are in order at this point:

- Baseline statistics and observation are two entries into what people really do. For the most part, most people do not change much. (Why was the internet an exception?)
- Again, begin your analysis of possibilities with what is known about what people really do. There are exceptions, but most successful innovations in some way improve the experience of what people are doing now rather than require radical change of timetables, skills, associations, or satisfactions.
- If some change would be required, look hard at assertions that people will change. Why? What would be a powerful enough inducement to change? What would have to be given up? What would be the barriers to adopting something new? Change comes hard for most people most of the time. There are exceptions, but why this one?

Case

Apply the questions above to the awesome expansion of the electronic game industry. What characteristics made it an exception to the conservative and cautionary warnings?

Hint: Did it enhance or transform established habits and contexts?

There is this complex and ongoing case of electronics and miniaturization. The technical innovations are great and continual. I can hold in my hand more power than would have filled a room at the beginning of my academic career. Nanotechnology, they tell us, will make everything electronic faster, smaller, more portable, and more powerful . . . in months not years.

Along with this comes communication possibilities. Computing is one thing. Calculating is possible for anything binary. There is excitement, accessibility, and immediacy in connecting electronically. There are also considerable risks. For those who love game playing, the expansion of opportunity is exciting and wildly attractive. It is, in the terms we have been using, an engrossing, challenging, and flow-inducing experience. Of course, the development and expansion is literally exponential.

But is it real? Many questions have yet to be answered about diversion from other kinds of learning, other more direct ways of connecting,

---

and saturation in appeal that calls for ever new devices and programs. Perhaps the limitations are more significant. We are embodied physical and material beings who do not live entirely in the mind. The mind-body relationship seems unbreakable and essential. We are also social beings. What happens on the court or course, in the outdoors, in the rhythm and touching of dance, and in the bedroom cannot be reproduced electronically. (As far as I know.) All leisure experiences cannot be enabled with any device or program, even with representations in 3-D. The fact that we are embodied suggests one approach to RB investment that is unlikely to disappear.

Debate

A class might want to argue both sides of this analysis. (After all, the author is not a 21st century teen.)

The Big Case

The multiple Walt Disney Worlds (WDWs) are far too big and complex to make a case study. However, a few hints may be in order, but none substitute for actually being there *and* observing. Sitting on a bench and watching what people are doing, whom they are with, and their moods and expressions is really instructive. There are also many analyses of the history and development of the WDWs online. Check them out.

Is everything a tale of success? Cultural context makes a difference. Disneyland Paris did not gain the same acceptance (market) as Orlando or Japan. Why not?

One consistent complaint was long lines and waiting, even with Mickey and a princess entertaining nearby. So, ever alert, the operators at the design center developed a smartphone design for estimating wait times and tickets that gave priority to a limited number of sites. The gradual incorporation of research-based adjustments has been an interesting development. (The moral: Nothing is perfect and continual evaluation research is necessary, even at WDW.)

For Those Who Have Been There

Discuss your experience highs and lows. For those interested in corporate development, the history of how Disney developed from a virtual monarchy, to an oligarchy, to a modern corporation is fascinating. When I first did a little on-site research at WDW, they were proud of doing no

> market research and believed they already knew how to develop their assets. There have been big changes in the almost 40 years since my first visit, including in-house research and marketing packages of travel, accommodations, and passes.

CHAPTER 12:
THE LITTLE PICTURE

Some of the hype about small business is a bit deceptive. It is unquestioned that over half fail in less than two years. Most failure estimates are higher. Touted as job creators, about half of small businesses employ no one. They are staffed entirely by their owners and/or the owner's family. This includes many recreation businesses that are local and provide on-site services. Many are also seasonal.

Even small businesses face complications. They report revenues and pay taxes. If they have employees, they become involved in reporting employee incomes and paying payroll taxes. Decisions regarding structure such as the choice between incorporation or a limited partnership may be made based on tax codes that can change at any time. Insurance, when obtainable, can be expensive. Other issues such as seasonality, location, competition, financing, and accounting require careful consideration.

Given all this, there remain possibilities that are exciting, are profitable, and possess growth potential. In this chapter, we explore some of the possibilities. This will not, however, be a catalog of the range of viable businesses, but a set of perspectives from which we can develop a strategy.

Target Markets Revisited

One type of target market is national or global. If the business is based on a particular activity-facilitating product, then it may best be marketed on the internet. Establishing a website, with or without the assistance of specialists (who can be found via search engines), is just the beginning. The website should feature how and why the product is different. Text and pictures should be oriented to those who are in the 20 to 25% who do the activity regularly. In some cases, the product may enhance the experience for almost anyone who does the base activity. In more cases, it will improve the experience for those already adept and dedicated.

The big advantage of this business strategy is its low cost. Hooking up with services such as PayPal, targeted websites, and a reliable distribution service can keep initial costs confined to the development and production of the item (along with patenting if advisable). In some cases, the market may be so specific that narrowly focused journals and outlets will reach a high proportion of the target. In others, more Web ingenuity is required.

The focus of promotion should always be on what the product does to enhance the play experience. Such promotion is best designed by those who know the nature of that experience. However, it is important that we seek a range of those who do the activity rather than assume that our own approach is universal.

The local business is located at the other end of the market spectrum. It may be located in the center of a set of users who then take their purchases to a variety of locations. Or it may be at or near a prime site for doing the activity. In either case, location is critical. A side street or failing strip mall may offer a tempting rental. However, the savings in rent will often be more than offset by the costs of promotion. Even a good billboard can run more than rental savings.

Many successful leisure businesses are "piggybacks." That is, they provide a useful service near a prime activity site such as a beach, ski slope, rock face, public facility, school or college, or whatever draws participants. Again, a careful assessment of the size and accessibility of the target market is required. A unique or different service may create new market possibilities, but those old baseline numbers are important for any strategy.

The core of a marketing strategy is the experience. The questions of what people do, how they do it, and how choices are made have to be asked and answered from as many sources of information and analysis as possible. Promotion and location follow trying to answer these often hard questions. The remainder of this chapter offers clues to answering these questions.

Specialties: Small Markets and Surprising Profits

Back to those specialty activities that have a small number of regular participants, usually less than .5 of 1% of the adult population, but still offer viable markets in the right time and place. Some specialties require a special environment that may draw amateurs (i.e., lovers of the activity) to that special location. There are specialties such as windsurfing and sailing in the Columbia River Gorge, soaring near hilly terrain with wind, climbing at rock faces, and certain backcountry activities.

Case: How Long Is the Indoor Season?

One surprising enterprise was begun by a mountain biker in the snow belt. No doubt listening to the complaints of his fellow bikers, he developed a concept for an indoor mountain bike park in the Milwaukee area. A number of factors worked for him. One was a concentration of outdoor off-road bikers in the area. A second was the availability of large warehouse-type buildings empty due to the recession. A third was his technical knowledge that enabled him to design a complex and varied set of runs. The fourth was a strategy that took into account that this was a counter-season business, so income had to be gained in that season, 4 to 6 months depending on weather.

This strategy was based on the entrepreneur's intimate knowledge of the sport and what made it attractive. However, even in Wisconsin the market was limited to the core participants in a low-numbers activity. It was a niche market for a niche activity. One indication of the validity of the scheme is the distances some come to use the facility. Would it work elsewhere? Not in many locations. Is the sport at the peak of its activity life cycle? The answer to this question would require careful research.

Research: Are there any niche businesses in your area? How did the entrepreneur assess the potential market? Did the entrepreneur envision a growth market? Why?

There are, no doubt, other niche possibilities. Some are local. Some require a careful assessment of the numbers of dedicated clients with feasible access to the location. Initial analysis includes specialty dedicated markets, flow experience and the conditions that enable it, and possible organizations of related amateurs and their locations. Are there risks? Of course, but such niche markets may be among the most reliable when fads are recognized and avoided.

Joint Use: An Economical Strategy

In many instances, a speciality business can economize by renting public or multiuse space in an existing location. For example, in a suburban planned community center, an incredible variety of activities were offered, some by entrepreneurs. The center included a small theater, a pool, a woodworking shop, a dance studio, and classrooms. Even the pool could be rented at dedicated times. Other activities included the following:

- Drawing, painting, sculpture, printmaking, and woodworking classes
- Performing arts with acting, ballet, jazz dance, guitar, African dance, and yoga
- Cooking, photography, fiber, and ceramics classes
- Tryout groups such as "dance for klutzes"—a step at a time
- Special aquatics including water ballet
- Visiting performances and concerts

The point is that a recreation business (RB) can be started and market-tested in such community centers and other rental spaces with investment costs limited. Of course, personal time and marketing are not free. Economists call it opportunity cost—time and income that might have been used for one's leisure or other income production. But the opportunity can be worth the cost!

Issue

How can an entrepreneur avoid being overenthusiastic about an activity in which he or she is deeply involved?

At the center of such markets is the devotion of clients to the activity. Many are the amateurs who define themselves within the activity. They often devote remarkable portions of their income to the activity, even placing housing and clothing in distant second place. There has long been a recognition of devotees who are "horse poor." Maybe there are those who are "Harley poor," "book or art poor," or even "golf poor."

Big Markets in Small Places

Contrasting niche markets for activities with small numbers are special opportunities for large-number activities. It is the if-you-build-it-they-will-come myth. However, the field of dreams can turn into the sinkhole of nightmares. Again, beware of promoters such as those who have hawked sports arenas in mid-sized cities with promises of attracting growth and ancillary investment. Many arenas now sit largely empty and devour tax dollars, not entirely victims of a recession. Among other factors ignored were operating costs, difficulties of attracting home teams, and the constant competition of sports on television.

Nevertheless, there are big-number niches. Many depend on special environments. For example, even with golf courses closing and country clubs bankrupt, a stunning design in a gorgeous location operated at modest cost may attract those tired of urban crowds and membership pressures at the private club. Of course, overbuilding in a boom and failure to recognize that peaks are followed by declines can lead to failure. If you build it, they may go somewhere else or just not do it.

The major draw for a business based on large-participation activities is the base numbers. A specialty activity may have only 100,000 players across the country. An activity such as golf may have over 20 million; bowling, 25 million; running/jogging, 32 million; and tennis, over 10 million (U.S. Census Bureau, 2011). Even when we apply the 80–20 rule on frequency, that's a lot of people. Numbers for gardening, reading, and walking are even higher. Then there are over 65 million boaters, 12 million hunters, 25 million freshwater fishers, and 60 million visits to ski slopes (U.S. Census Bureau, 2011). That's a lot of people, even when we recognize some declines during a recession and glutted markets for resale boats and other recreation items.

The catch is, of course, competition. Competition is everywhere. For equipment and apparel, there are the big boxes and the small boxes (online). In many areas, so many destination resorts have been developed that markets are saturated and savvy investors are looking for the twice-bankrupt at fire-sale prices. "One more" in many market areas may be one too many. Three successful businesses in an area may saturate the market, so the fourth will flop.

However, opportunities are available for the clever and resourceful who know the nature of the base activity:

- One opportunity involves analyzing what the big businesses do not offer around the edges. Supplementary services may do well near the big resort, near federal or state recreation areas including wilderness access points, or as a regional supplier of high-end items for which quality is paramount in buying decisions.
- Another opportunity is high-quality instruction in an activity, again in a location where markets are of adequate size. You do not have to own a tennis complex to gain a reputation as the best teaching pro around, a concert hall to teach piano or woodwinds, a boatyard to renovate older models, or a factory to specialize in the Harley or Sekai brands, but you do need to be in the right location.
- The best facility may not be the biggest. We may find it impossible to compete with the big guys at the major locations, but what about small ski slopes near a city, a ceramics studio for

those out of school, or a small fitness center near a large working population who can get out of the office or lab for an hour at odd times?

There are online specialty outlets for walkers and joggers who require high-quality and carefully designed shoes; adapted chairs for "wheelie" sports; and travel organizers for clients with specialty interests, preferably with discretionary income to spend. The trick is knowing the activity, the modes of participation, and the nature of related experiences. The big businesses are not always good at details.

Competition means that if you build it, someone else may already be there. Expanding a business is usually cheaper than starting a new one. Plus an established recreation-based business already has a hold on a significant market share.

One strategy is building on someone else's success somewhere else. Identifying successful businesses and their strategies can be a big head start for a different location. Again, it is crucial that we analyze the market base.

Another strategy is building on someone else's failure. A good concept may be ruined by poor operation or inadequate financing. Failure is a big warning, but there are times at which and places where a business can be purchased or leased at a discount and renewed by management that has identified problems that can be remedied.

Questions

Question 1

What are some second-chance RB successes?

Clue: Look first at major market areas.

Question 2

How can businesses that have saturated a market be identified?

Clue: Unfulfilled markets can be identified based on scheduling issues in an existing RB.

Dilemmas of Design and Operation

One balancing act for a leisure business is between the security of a no-surprises approach versus the challenge of something new and different. From a flow perspective, a regular and even familiar context may be essential to achieving a high level of involvement. Wild winds can disrupt the skill–challenge pairing in an outdoor sport. In indoor settings, disruptive activity in the area can prevent full concentration. Management of a recreation environment requires attention to the regular conditions that enhance the experience.

On the other hand (again), too much familiarity can produce boredom. Making the same ceramics bowl over and over, playing the same opponent for a year, or hiking the same trail 50 times can deteriorate a good experience.

Uniqueness versus familiarity can be a dilemma in RB design and operation. How can an artificial climbing wall not become boring? How can a theme park not become too familiar? Of course, finding new challenge is largely up to the client. The client can seek new opponents or companions, try different techniques, learn new skills, and take risks in the recreation process. It is important for the business provider to control disruptive or overutilized environments while enabling new experiences and challenges. Grading the difficulty of ski slopes and trails is a clue to such management.

Question

Are there ways to achieve a balance between reliability and novelty in leisure settings?

Hint: Strategies may involve other people as well as design.

The next chapter offers some perspectives on management that enhances the client's experience. For the most part, it is based on research into recreation experiences and satisfactions. However, it is probably worthwhile to remind ourselves that we need to watch and listen carefully when clients are coming, playing, and leaving, for indications of them having had a great time. Watching can be unobtrusive. Occasionally, a follow-up question after an expression of satisfaction can guide the manager to an improved operation. "Watch and listen" is not just for crossing the street.

Competition Around the Edges

When exploring the small-business scene, we can often find opportunities around the edges. That is, a major set of activities or provisions may involve a sizable market that is not being fully met. For example, a burgeoning youth soccer program may need servicing for equipment, repairs, instruction in the off-season, or even tournament transportation. Some markets seem more than adequately met by the big boxes, but we cannot be too sure. Gardening supplies and equipment inventories from the big guys tend to be regional or even national. The special requirements of a local area can often be missed.

The point is that activities that involve a lot of people are not necessarily supported in all aspects by established businesses, however sophisticated their computer systems. How do we locate such edge opportunities? Probably by counting the base numbers and then observing and asking. Often, such niche markets are known best by those already involved in the activity and locale. A warning, however, may be in order. Do not get carried away by your own enthusiasm to project an everyone-will-want-to-do-it approach.

Who Isn't There: Research on Not Doing It

I'll have to be honest here. Not much research attention has been given to not engaging in any leisure activity. However, there has been some study of blocking and inhibiting factors. Some are self-evident and need no more than mention here. Others may be a bit more tricky.

The Big Blockages: Time and Money

Many people who would like to take up an activity or do it more do not have the time. In one study in Oregon, I interviewed a single mom of three children who was running a restaurant and whose 8 a.m. to midnight schedule did not include anything done for anticipated satisfaction in doing it. She may have been an extreme, but lack of predictable time for discretionary activity is the most common blockage for leisure engagement.

As suggested, there are ways of responding to this problem. The first is flexible operation schedules. The second is identifying time-starved people who could be accommodated with some programmatic adjustments and innovations. The third is designing and locating for time efficiency. Some clients want a place to hang out, whereas others want to have a quick in and out. Both markets are important.

> ### Research
>
> By observation and/or experience, try to identify time-pressured clients versus socializing players at a locale or facility. What factors differentiate them? How can an RB respond to such a difference?

The money issue is somewhat different. A large proportion of the population simply cannot afford much if any recreation with significant cost. In a study of laid-off steelworkers, Lisa Raymond (1985) found that one of the first things they gave up was going to major league ball games, despite the free time forced on them. However, there are ways of meeting even this blocker. Some low-income clients have time flexibility and can become secondary markets for off-peak hours at reduced cost. Unfortunately, as more economic sectors have schedules similar to schools and other retailers, more peak time is overlapping than separate. Everyone, including students, wants the 5 to 10 p.m. playing times in the late afternoons and evenings. Flex schedules among some retailers and services can open times that can be offered at cut prices.

It is evident that time and money frequently combine to be a double barrier to leisure engagement.

Social Factors

Many activities are done with groups rather than alone. Generally, these groups are not made up of strangers. A leisure business can frequently enlarge markets in two ways. One is facilitating participation by natural groups such as families and work associates. A second is providing opportunities, often no more complex than a coffee and conversation area in which clients can meet and develop relationships. (If this seems to contradict the time scarcity problem, it is only a reminder that markets for the same activity in the same place may be varied.) And on-site child care is not outmoded, regardless of changing household configurations.

Another social factor in many activities is skill level. Especially in sports, programs are differentiated by skill level designated by number schemes, labels, or other symbols. In individual sports, the issue is met by "ladders" in which participants may move up or down and enhance competition. In other cases, there are labeled groupings. (Preferably not "Bluebirds" and "Robins.") In any case, managers need to be alert to incorporate players who are hesitant to risk being misplaced or embarrassed by lack of skill. Just being welcoming and inclusive does not solve the problem.

Leisure and the "New" Urban Associations

A counter-market is found mostly in urban areas where there are lots of strangers, people not tied into social networks. Many different kinds of activity can be venues for meeting others. An important factor is that a recreation setting brings together people with at least one thing, and often several things, in common. Churches used to provide such a social setting, and still do for some. Now, however, in this time of "unmarried-ness," leisure serves the same purpose for many. For the RB manager, providing times and places for interacting may be more important for attracting and retaining clients than the efficiency of getting people in and out fast. There is a whole new industry of helping people meet that may be more successful in places of mutual activity than on the World Wide Web.

Issue

Imagine an RB in which some clients want to meet and interact with interesting new friends and partners, whereas others do not want the sexual interaction hassles. Can both be accommodated?

Clue: Scheduling can help, but space is usually limited.

Added complication: Recreation venues are not exempt from sexual harassment.

Learning Skills and Gaining Satisfactions

Note the overlap here with the previous concept. Generally, as skills increase in any activity, so do satisfactions. Near the top of most lists of "why I don't do. . ." is a lack of skill. Most business providers of recreation activity have learning programs central to their overall offering. But they may find it difficult to provide upgrades as well as introductions. They have to know the skills of an activity well to calibrate upgrades and offer them in ways attractive to their clients. However, they have a second-ary benefit in increasing participation. These upgrades build personal satisfactions in skill development and potential flow and bring together activity associates of similar levels of advancement.

In the next chapter, we focus on client-focused management with some of the issues and possibilities of this chapter as background.

Special Case: A Local Business History

A recent graduate of a liberal arts college in Oregon had worked in retail to pay his way through college and get started as a "young mar-ried" after graduation. The men's clothing store where he was a popular salesman had a dead-end future since it was owner operated. However, he recognized that in a town about 30 miles from the city, there might be a different opportunity. There would be no local competition for a store that carried a general line of sporting goods aimed especially at the student market.

First, there was the issue of location. Fortunately, a small store a half block from the front of the campus was unoccupied. It was too small and the building needed rehabbing, but it was convenient and low cost. Then, there was the issue of financing. The budding entrepreneur was known by the local bank officers, who provided a line of credit based on the business plan and the known character of the proposer.

There were some surprises. What was the biggest profit line? Shoes. All sorts of shoes. What else developed? School sports in a growing area were a market for equipment and even uniforms, but those contracts called for careful calculations to beat the competition with a profit margin. What product caused the most problems? Returns of defective product from the famous brand of athletic shoes whose headquarters was only a few miles away.

The biggest management problem? The time required. This relatively small store required sales hours, inventory assessment and records, bookkeeping, tax reporting, employee training, and cleaning up. It was a 6.5 day workweek for years, not easy for a young father who took parenting seriously.

He had a major decision to make after a few years when a much larger store space became available. First, the rent would be an increased fixed expense. Second, it was a block further from the campus and not as much on student routes. Third, it would require a bigger investment of stock and sales personnel. However, the risks came with a much increased business volume and with reducing the number of times that inquiries had to be met with "we don't carry that."

This introduction illlustrates how such an analytical history can be a project for the student of RB. At this point, the student might question how the entrepreneur dealt with later sets of issues. What are the elements that would have affected such a business?

The climate of even a local retail business may be affected by the following:

1. Big-box sports stores that are parts of chains with their mass buying power, regional and national advertising, proven formulas for stocking and market assessment, and access to financing.
2. The move of chain superstores such as Walmart into sporting goods. Personal service may be limited, but the trade-off is price at levels no local store can match. Manufacturers even produce

low-price sports equipment with the same name brands that are on the quality products.
3. The convenience of online shopping with almost any item at a competitive price purchased in minutes from the comfort of the home and the simplicity of the laptop.

Would that small retail store have a chance? What would have been your prediction 1, 2, or 3 decades ago and in the face of competition from all sides and angles?

Let's close with the good news. As of 2017, our entrepreneur is comfortably retired having sold the business, but retained the two buildings as investments. His word to those considering such a retail recreation-based business? It can be done, but plan on a lot of personal investment in time, energy, thought, planning, and being there.

CHAPTER 13:
SERVICING THE EXPERIENCE

Is experience a commodity, something that can be designed, labeled, packaged, and sold in the same way for all consumers? Or is it changing, shifting, and even individualized? The answer is clearly the latter. Delivery of the possibility of leisure experience is a process, not a product. Therefore, recreation business (RB) is a kind of service industry with client-oriented management that is constantly sensitive to what is occurring and not occurring.

The theater metaphor previously mentioned (Pine & Gilmore, 1999) is useful in its focus on performance and the reception of the client. It suggests that in a leisure context there are many roles to be played. The focus, however, is on the receivers who also are active in the process. Recreation experience is never just reception, passive. It is an involving process in which the players are all acting in one way or another. The business managers are not just presenting, but are making possible the roles of active participation. In the end, the aim is peak experiences for the clients.

One implication is that the provider roles may vary. Some engage closely with the players in enhancing the experience. Others provide an environment and stay out of the way. In any case, we aim to maximize the involvement and satisfaction of the clients. This chapter provides an analysis from a wide range of research on elements of satisfying leisure experiences and ways of enhancing them.

Components of Leisure Experience

One question concerns how we can gain an understanding of the components of good recreation experiences. How can we sum up a process that may go on for hours or even days? Almost all questionnaire research assumes that at the end of an event or even days later in response to a written or online set of questions, the recreation participant can sum up the quality of the event or environment. The obvious problem is that any experience of duration will rise and fall in satisfaction, even from minute to minute. Summations are not usually a good way to sort out and identify the components that produce highs and lows. Questionnaires have value, but they are too abstract to tap immediate elements. Further, a lot of research notes how the order, wording, and context of summation questions can radically influence responses. Nonetheless, because recollections can provoke return business, they can be useful.

A second approach is experience sampling. It involves using a device to interrupt whatever is going on at random times so respondents can answer questions about right now. Of course, one immediate problem is that the experience is already interrupted rather than ongoing. However, it avoids many of the problems of the summation of, "On the whole, how would you rate your visit to the . . . ?"

Experience sampling has often focused on the question of when people are happiest. The management clues that follow are based to a large extent on the findings of such an approach. We have already noted that people tend to be most satisfied when they are active rather than passive, when they are in the flow of skill and challenge, and when they are with people with whom they have positive ongoing relationships. These findings are consistent across almost any kind of recreation environment and activity. However, probably no two kinds of activity or settings facilitate these satisfactions in the same way, not to mention for different people.

Managing for Experience

Can flow be manufactured? Can we organize an event so people enjoy each other? Are meanings and emotions programmable? The answer is "not really." No program can guarantee any particular result when real people are involved, especially people in groups. Any individual comes to an occasion with a complex set of histories, evoked emotions, and idiosyncrasies. Group interaction is a process in which combinations of actions and reactions create ever new environments. The quality of the experience is emergent, not predetermined.

However, there are research-based clues about how we can enhance experiences and maximize positive outcomes. Such clues also can help us avoid negative outcomes. These clues concern designed environments, approaches to enabling an experience, and a few programmatic possibilities. Experience is, by definition, to a great extent open ended. We may refer to RB providers, but more accurately they are enablers. Nevertheless, many designs, styles, communication modes, and responses can make a difference. Some no doubt will be found in entrepreneurial texts, often with somewhat different vocabularies. In this case, we begin with the social and behavioral studies.

The End Effect

Kahneman (2011) reports research that has found that end effects have disproportionate weight in evaluating an experience. The entire event contributes to evaluation, and high and low points may occur at any time. However, the ending is especially significant. We cannot control events so that every participant wins the last point, receives the final applause, or has the final product rise above the quality norm. If it could be externally manipulated, it would thwart the uncertainties that are central to many recreation experiences. However, some elements would apply to almost any business management approach.

Tour operators do not offer a closing dinner out of generosity. That final event allows travelers to reinforce each other in recalling the high points of a trip. The risk is that discomforts and conflicts may be recalled as well. However, the strategy of designing a program toward an ending with highs is almost always a good one.

In an indoor provision, attention can be given to the leaving experience. Personal recognition and return affirmations are always good. Managers should instill on their front desk personnel the importance of arrivals and departures met with smiles, name recognition, and, when possible, a personal element.

The design aspects of the end-stage experience are probably less commonly recognized. How many leisure providers skimp on aspects such as chat areas and shower and changing spaces? Can a great game have a reduced impact in a dingy shower or a smelly locker room? Of course, cold showers can lead to frozen faces and chilled memories.

This does not have to mean extra expense or making it fancy. I did a user survey at an indoor tennis facility some years ago when the operator was thinking about upgrading the space at considerable cost. The overwhelming results of the survey were that the players wanted the most tennis at the lowest viable cost. Their priority for improvement was better lighting in the play area to enhance the central experience, rather than an upgraded foyer. Nevertheless, attention to departures can yield high returns on the dollar.

Related to this is knowing when not to sell. A positive experience can be alloyed by a persistent effort to sell at the departure. We want clients to remember how good they felt on the way home, not an annoyance or intrusion. In this economic culture where efforts to promote and sell are continual, discretion and judgment regarding when *not* to sell may be as important as developing an attractive promotion program.

> **Question**
>
> What are the most important departure elements in your RB concept?
> Recall and share a really good departure experience from your own life.
> **Clue:** Distinguish the personal from the environmental.

Leisure Is Personal

At the beginning, a design that symbolizes welcome can often be obtained with minimal expense. Spaces that are welcoming are open and light and have meeting areas. Personal greetings are important for anyone, especially for those who are new or hesitant.

Almost all recreation businesses are dealing with people in groups of varying sizes and compositions. In some cases, all who come together will play together. More often, activity groups meet at the site, so meeting spaces are crucial. They should be open and accessible, not hard to locate, and with décor and furnishings that signal welcome and social inclusion. The details will vary with the activity, social groupings, and space that is adaptable. But the central aim is facilitating gathering.

> **Research**
>
> Evaluate on-site or recall your arrival at a recreation site. What environmental elements are welcoming? Note signage, lighting, open doors, steps, colors, and a clear sight line to the desk. What about personal factors such as greetings, clothing of personnel, name recognition, and readiness to help? Which factors make the client feel immediately welcome and important?

The Dropout Problem

Research suggests at least two partial responses to the constant problem of clients who begin a program and then disappear. One is social and the second endemic to the play experience. The dropout rate in many programs exceeds 80% in relatively short periods. Exercise and fitness centers commonly have dropout rates so high that some develop pricing programs to get as much money as possible up front with the likelihood that they may not have to provide time and space for most new clients in a few weeks or months. Assuming that the long-term success of a business is better served by retaining clients, what can we do to improve retention rates?

The first strategy is social. Recreation participants are most likely to stay in programs and not to miss regular times when they are part of a group. There are double factors: the positive enjoyment of the group and meeting their expectations. Anything we can do to encourage and facilitate the formation of play groups with a regular schedule will reduce dropouts and absentees. Of course, in competitive sports for which numbers are essential, the social factor is especially salient. Making it convenient to reserve regular times and giving group discounts may pay off for the business.

Issue

Is social commitment best left to clients? How can a manager encourage regular groupings without forcing incompatible clients together? Any examples?

Clue: It is not difficult for us to enable commitment to regularity by providing a system of time reservations, easy group formation, and help with contingencies.

The second strategy is based on the research of Ed McAuley of the University of Illinois. He has repeated studies demonstrating that experiencing efficacy is central to continuing an activity. This means simply that people tend to stay with an activity in which they feel they do well and/or are improving their skills. Goals should be challenging but reachable. This ties into the flow approach for skill-based activities. For others, the goals may be other outcomes such as health and fitness or social recognition.

Examples

Efficacy is partly analytical, partly the recognition of others, and partly just a feeling. No simple program can guarantee such a self-evaluation. But how can we enlarge the opportunity? (Personal examples may be helpful at this point.)

Problem: The common method of rewards (ribbons, medals, etc.) has the problem that recognizing "winners" disrespects "losers," who may be most of the group. Youth sports have attempted to deal with this problem with the everyone-is-a-winner approach and mass distribution of medals and plaques. Does this work, or does it make the whole approach meaningless?

Clue: Is personal affirmation better than a reward program?

In both cases, management involves more than providing an opportunity and stepping aside. Effective management involves being there and recognizing how experiences can be enhanced and consolidated.

Who Is Acting?

It is not cynical to recognize that in a sense everyone is putting on a show. That is, everyone is presenting a kind of self in ways that will create desirable responses from others. We not only think about appearance, but even more choose how we speak, respond, and interact with some sense of how others will see us and respond. Implications for the front-line personnel of an RB are obvious. However, it is also part of the leisure experience for clients.

The idea is not that a recreation site should be managed so that people can show off, at least not too much. However, opportunities for some display can add to the positive experience. In an arts program, we can grade rotating displays and programs of affirmation in ways that give recognition to improvement. In sports, it is a bit trickier. Leader boards and rankings have bottoms as well as tops that may discourage engagement. Careful attention to improvement at any level of skill and interaction that calls attention to intrinsic satisfaction can enhance the experience for beginners and the less adept.

The sometimes hidden point is that people are constantly looking at the responses of others and finding satisfaction when they seem positive. Any activity participant knows to take opportunities to applaud and encourage others, especially those in the lower end of the learning curve. The serving personnel of a business should seek out and create opportunities for such responses.

Is Everyone a Winner?

Of course, all this can go too far. For a learner to be overpraised or unrealistically evaluated renders the attempt meaningless. However, it is a primary task of RB service personnel to look for legitimate opportunities for approval, as well as to design the program so that there can be successes at any level. And the more spontaneous the approval, the more authentic it seems.

The following words and phrases, along with body language and tonal inflection, should be drilled into front-line recreation service providers at any level:

- "Great . . . job, shot, or anything else!"
- "Looking good out there today!"

- "Everyone enjoys playing with you!"
- "Remember the good days (results, product) when things don't go quite so well."
- "Always good to see you come through that door!"

Affirmation can come in many forms. Sometimes, a good smile says more than words. "Wow" may say more than an analysis of a good production or result. Those who say this are not being phony, but being the kind of companion that often makes or breaks an experience. Remember that it is the experience you are selling, not just the activity itself.

Question

Come up with an affirming approach that would work for your business.

Hint: Different strokes for different folks.

Clue: Everyone isn't a winner . . . or can they be?

Beyond Hedonism

One of my colleagues complained years ago at the failure of those who study leisure and recreation to employ the term *fun*. It was a point well taken. Complex analysis of motivations and satisfactions may obscure that many choices are just an anticipation of having fun. Kahneman (2011) is right that System 2 analysis of interrelated meaning dimensions is unlikely in most recreation decisions.

However, having fun may be more than an emotion. Rather, the emotion seems to be a consequence of some elements of an experience. A continual question for a recreation manager is, what did I do or could I do to support my clients having fun? Then we are immediately into trying to understand what that experience can be and how a business design and operation can enhance those positive factors. Satisfaction does not just happen, even in play. Rather, it is a process with components that rise and fall in significance. Summation evaluations often fail to identify the more immediate elements. In fact, even experience sampling that takes random slices of a total process is as likely to miss the peaks and valleys as not. That is why we need to be sensitive to any and every clue that could point to a managerial improvement.

Opportunity Outside the Box

I will not belabor the importance of critical observation again except to put it at the front of the line of information-gathering techniques. Some clues may also help us understand what is really going on out there.

First, in observation there is the problem of a false focus. If we focus only on the "official" activity, such as learning, competing, or producing something, we may miss the "side bets" that are of major importance in the total experience. We have already suggested what many of them may be. Most are usually social, interaction in and around the central activity. Others may be more specific to the nature of an activity. Experimenting, exploring, and otherwise trying out new ways of engagement are significant to many people. Environments that encourage trying things out by minimizing the costs of failure can lead to new peaks. Just getting away into a different environment can be important, especially for those who feel home- or office-bound. Just playing the game is not all that is going on.

Second, there is the question of what people are *not* doing and would like to do. Observation is probably of less help here. Sometimes we can see clients try out unconventional ways of engagement that suggest boredom. However, relaxed post-experience conversations that introduce a question that many people never consider can also be useful. "I wonder if there is another way to do this?" may encourage participants to share that offbeat idea that they have been harboring and are reluctant to share. Some ideas are impossible or unlikely to produce a better experience. But all are worth listening to. Conversely, "this is the way we do it here, take it or leave it" can turn off many clients.

Third, beware of survey results claiming interest. In neighborhood questionnaires, large numbers of respondents will answer that they would like a new swimming pool, running track, bicycle trail, or whatever. However, when these facilities are built, few people will change their habits and investments to become regular clients. Of course, there is the matter of price. At some unrealistically low price, lots of people will do almost anything. But this is of little use to an entrepreneur. All sorts of activities look potentially attractive when we do not have to consider what we would have to change, give up, or rearrange to do it. This does not mean that surveys are useless, but that we always have to be put them in the context of baseline numbers of what people are doing now.

Fourth, look around . . . even far away. There are clues out there in what people are doing and how they do it that may lead to good business concepts. When older people bike in inconvenient and even risky places, they may be indicating a latent demand. When people travel to do something, they may be suggesting a market for something similar nearby. When older people no longer do something they had enjoyed earlier, they may have been forced out by circumstances or even ageist prejudices and be a market for renewal. Of course, asking about what might increase participation or get them back into something discontinued is always a possibility. Look and listen, and try to lay prejudices aside.

Question

Considering the demographics of your market area, what might be a new opportunity for a target market?

Clue: First, check for population shifts such as age, household composition, or education level.

Market Segmentation

Can an RB attract an inclusive clientele, or is it better for an RB to target and focus? One issue is that potential conflicts between market segments may drive potential clients away. Some have already been suggested: teen play versus adult lap-swimming in a pool, loud music versus quiet time, and any other conflicting styles of recreation. On a big beach, there can be programmed and self-selected segregation. Other environments are adaptable. However, focus on one market segment may drive away viable paying clients who seek a somewhat different experience. Again, careful observation may spot potential conflicts before they cost too many clients.

Problem

List again the potential market segments for your proposed business. Do you see possible conflicts in style and desired experience? If so, in what ways can you minimize the conflicts and protect the desired experience?

The often-hidden issue: Recreation environments, as suggested before, can become sites for unwanted interaction, that is, sexual harassment. Again observation is important, but solutions short of segregation may be difficult. (Here class discussion or written case histories that are shared online may be valuable *if* they are received with sensitivity.) Also, remember that one bad experience can drive away a client forever.

Associative Memory and Marketing

RB marketing is usually specific to the activity base, population characteristics, and location. The old tourism three *S*s of sun, sand, and sex do not even do it for tourism anymore. However, some clues in the social psychology of decision making can be useful.

Kahneman (2011) analyzes associative memory in decisions, especially the less analytical System 1 kind. What do we remember from a really satisfying experience? As already suggested, usually the highs and lows, the endings, and the companions. Those key recollections vary according to the experience: the social and physical environment, the nature of the activity, and the level of involvement. In marketing strategies, we clearly aim to call up the positive elements and repress the negative.

How do we remember? In the process of associative memory, signs and symbols are "tags" for elements of a total experience. Generally, when we recall a leisure, or any other, occasion, it is in relatively simple images, words and phrases, and delineated segments of the total. We do not go through a complex experience sorting out the positive from the negative in a hierarchical schema.

When trying to attract clients, new or repeat, we aim to identify and employ those symbols and vocabularies that tap the highs of satisfaction and do not inadvertently trigger negatives. Print and Web advertising employ pictures that not only attract attention but also direct consciousness to positive associations. To do this, we need to know the nature of the experience thoroughly. It is unlikely that an ad expert who is only a consumer rather than someone involved will be able to do this. However, the requirements are much the same as those for good management.

The trick is identifying those words and images that call forth the positive associations, especially the highs. For tourism, they may be what is called to mind by the properly populated beach. Attractive people are usually a good sign. However, they should not be extraordinary to the extent that they scare off clients. (Too many bikini models may not attract the mother who is making the destination choices.) The more the associations are specific to a business offering, the better. However, some businesses provide access or enhancement of an experience with another environment whose depiction calls up the desired associations.

Again, the focus is on the experience and its special positive associations. And the center of management and marketing is *quality*.

Project

Design an online ad for your prospective business.

Warning: Any ad can turn off some prospective clients and attract other. Check the negatives and positives of your design and elements of attraction. (The class can be the first targets.)

A really hard one: Design a billboard for your business. Remember the speed of those passing by. How can few words or images create interest? For which target markets?

CHAPTER 14:
BEATING THE ODDS

The theme of this penultimate chapter is simple: quality, quality, quality! If you know what quality means for your RB strategy, then you can skip to the final chapter. However, there may be a few approaches you have not thought of yet.

Beyond Satisfaction: Something Special

Many resorts have come up with a value-added concept that has set them apart from the competition. One includes a Friday pig roast including family entertainment. Some include field trips to nearby historic or archaeological sites. Some have special themes related to a sport or type of entertainment. A few years ago, I developed a concept for a family resort that included protected children's activity programs that free parents for their golf or tennis, on-site play areas, pet-friendly rooms, well-maintained beach areas, and suites designed for multiple generations. (It turned out that the developer from previous successful experience marketed a "standard" housing project that in its attractive location has done well without any recreation emphasis.) However, buyers include very few households with school-age children.

Other types of recreation businesses can develop their own signature themes that not only are central to marketing, but also set them apart from similar businesses. Experienced tourism operators can seize on some aspect of their plans, often related to the destination environment rather than the travel itself. Local businesses, as already suggested, may analyze their target markets and develop a presentation that is specific in its appeal.

Most approaches are based on a thorough knowledge of their client base combined with understanding the site and activity combination they offer. We aim to develop something special. It is the opposite of buying into a franchise that directs an operation into well-proven provisions and styles that are essentially the same from one place to another. In fact, franchises require the local owner to do it their way and write their contracts to enforce their standards. The advantage is that clients know what to expect. The disadvantage is that the local business loses flexibility and the freedom to respond to local conditions and opportunities.

How can you identify the "something special" that will not only distinguish one business from others but maximize its draw and retention? Again, largely by observing your own business in action and also by visiting parallel businesses. Look for the sights and sounds of joy. Watch and listen. (Even put down this book and get out there where people are playing.)

The key concept is quality. Remember that no one has to do it. If the experience made possible by your business does not yield a high level of satisfaction, or fun, then in time it will fail. Looking good may get people in the door, but it will not bring them back.

Barriers to Satisfaction

Remember that almost all recreation businesses require clients to come back over and over. Further, the best advertising is person to person. "How did you decide to come to our *whatever*?" "I heard about it from a friend."

What barriers to satisfaction prevent clients from wanting to do it over and over?

- Not connecting with enjoyable associates, partners, opponents, and other people
- Being unable to gain or exercise needed skills
- Becoming bored, as the challenge level does not increase with skills
- Finding the environment unattractive
- Being unable to coordinate convenient schedules with availability
- Increases in costs that provoke cost–benefits analyses
- The attraction of a competing experience when the quality of the current one fades

Many, perhaps most, recreation experiences are a process. They are not static in skills, challenges, companions, or development. The same client who expresses a high level of satisfaction early in the process may be ready to move on and away from your business when there are no opportunities for a more complex or challenging experience. One of the appeals of the computerized games array is that there is always something new to try and experience . . . and usually at a reasonable price. Further, the technologies offer something better with each iteration. Those games have come a long way from the simple weapons-aiming chips of the early developments.

The quality that attracted clients may not retain the same people. Further, if there is disappointment, if promise is not fulfilled, then those who do not have to do it will disappear. Of course, that is everyone, and they will talk down your business in ways that no clever promotion can overcome for long.

The Fatal Bias

Kahneman (2011) describes the fatal bias in several ways. One is the halo effect that says that "If it's mine, it's got to be good." Just facts are no deterrent to those who are in love with anything from a new relationship to a business plan. It is difficult to stand back when you are in love, even with a plan that entails financial risk.

Kahneman (2011) also offers the problem of priming. Words, images, histories, or relationships prime our attitudes and judgments. We are predisposed to have a positive reaction to a proposition that comes packaged in positive recollections, images, symbols, slogans, or presenters. It may be sexist and ageist for a company to select attractive young women to peddle drugs to male doctors, but they do prime favorably. The problem in business strategies is that it may work against us. Associating a strategy with our personal histories, possibly even not remembered consciously, can bias evaluation and lead to a failure of critical System 2 thinking.

The trick is to recognize our own biases. However, if it were that easy, we would avoid the error and produce one success after another. Recalling the business failure rates alone ought to place us on guard against our favorable biases. One way of dealing with the fatal priming bias will be offered at the end of this chapter.

Mapping the Market

Any kind of critical analysis based on fact is good. Some facts are relatively easy to obtain; others can be costly.

Anyone developing a business strategy who does not get out there and examine successes and failures is doomed to add to those failure statistics. In the process, it is crucial that we distinguish experts from promoters. Of course, if our informant has something to sell, all colors of flags are waving. On the other hand, real enthusiasm is a positive clue.

One basic question is how to get a realistic assessment of the market. The first step involves measuring the market by using geographically relevant census data as to household composition in the likely market area.

Second, the Statistical Abstracts of the United States offer some form of trend data on many recreation activities. A basic problem, however, is that the totals are aggregate and tell almost nothing about frequency and duration. Remember the 80–20 rule for a realistic guide to those big numbers.

Third, for those who have a lot of money, major marketing organizations can do all sorts of analysis from good databases. The problem is that we are talking many thousands of dollars for even targeted analyses. The recreation trends analysis of several years ago (Kelly & Warnick, 1999) was based on an excellent yearly household survey that allowed for identification of a wide range of significant market-identifying indices. At that time, the data were made available to universities at trivial cost. No longer. However, major players with lots of financing can get such analysis from Experian Simmons or a similar market research organization. For example, SRI International has done major studies for hotel chains, airlines, and others with the money to spend. But the results are proprietary. (A colleague could not even show me the index.)

Good trend analysis is valuable from two perspectives. It gives a clue as to activities that have peaked and are on the downward curve of the activity life cycle. This is so important when the mass media tout some latest craze, with no contextual analysis. On the positive side, trend analysis from reliable data can help identify activities that have settled at a stable plateau or have solid growth base.

However, nothing substitutes for OPE—other people's experience. Getting out there with their own critical observation and fearless questions can open and close whole new worlds of opportunity for recreation businesses.

Who Wins? Risk Aversion or Optimistic Bias

It depends . . . on what? The underlying aim of a strategy is to beat the odds of failure. It is difficult and possibly counterproductive to begin with an attitude of probable failure. However, the odds are what they are. How can we balance risk assessment and optimism?

Kahneman (2011) and others have found that for the most part people tend to be risk aversive. A variety of decision experiments have demonstrated that many, maybe most, decisions involving money are not a rational assessment of risk versus gain. Avoiding loss is valued more than greater gain, even when the ratio is clearly in favor of the potential gain. Explanations vary, but the finding is consistent.

However, thousands of entrepreneurs take risks with their savings, time, reputations, and egos to begin or purchase businesses. Somehow a combination of factors overcomes risk aversion. Certainly a belief in the business concept and plan is fundamental. A reasonable hope for profit usually involves running sets of numbers. Added factors may be the satisfaction of being involved in a set of activities and with clients we enjoy, living in a desirable environment, and having a measure of autonomy. Nonetheless, courage and optimism that can overcome risk aversion needs to be supported by careful System 2 analysis.

Remember that there is also an optimistic bias. The halo of "it's my idea," association with positive experiences, and excitement of doing something new and self-expressive are all factors in taking risks. Such positive factors are necessary to evoke the necessary optimism and persistence. So, on balance, who wins? In what ways can System 2 help the entrepreneur assess risk and possibility?

Just for Fun ... Probably:
Murphy's Law Has Not Been Repealed

You remember Murphy's Law, which warns that if anything can go wrong, it will. In business, there are several corollaries such as the following:

- Everything takes longer than you plan.
- If several things could go wrong, the worst will be first.
- Left to themselves, things tend to go from bad to worse.
- Human beings regress toward being mean (for stats students only).
- Every solution creates new problems.
- Nature—and agents—seek the hidden flaw.
- Finally, Murphy was an optimist.

Are There Sources of Help?

I hope that those who are this far into the discussion have a number of clues. Some are focused on the concept and on the likelihood of offering experiences of quality with all of the elements previously introduced. Again, there is no substitute for *quality* in every aspect of the business. No quality, no experience. No experience, no market. No one has to do it, remember?

What are the sources of help in decision making? (Most have been covered already.)

1. Examine businesses in noncompetitive locations and query their managers.
2. Read this and other books for questions as well as answers.
3. Get help in running numbers of capital requirements, operating expenses, accounting and other services, insurance, taxes, and other fixed costs.
4. Be realistic in estimating how long it will take to build a solid clientele.

5. Assess all the limitations of seasonality, competition near and far, markets and access, pricing limitations in relation to markets, and, always, the baseline numbers.
6. Be realistic with those who represent sources of OPM (other people's money).

When it comes to specifics, all we can do in a book is raise the questions and suggest where some answers may be found. Every entrepreneur has to develop the answers for a specific time and place. One warning: The shocking finding in case studies of recreation-based businesses, especially small ones, is that few investors have done this. Especially when self-financed, plans that address the critical questions were found to be the exceptions.

Seasons and Problems

On an island in the north end of Lake Michigan 30 miles from the mainland, there has been a continual flow of business starts and a high rate of failure. Probably the consistent issue is the length of the season, especially for short-visit tourists and even for the second-home summer residents. The high season is about seven weeks. Shoulder seasons are a few weeks, mostly at the end of summer. Recognition of retirement-age markets are partly offset by difficulties in employment pools when colleges and schools begin. As a result, except for a few core businesses, businesses that offer recreation or nonessentials have usually lasted only a few seasons.

What are the solutions?
1. Figure the short season against costs before beginning.
2. Have a portable or secondary business elsewhere.
3. Go where there is a longer season and/or larger market.

Solution 1 entails high prices. Solution 2 calls for personal versatility and flexibility. Solution 3 looks promising. Go to Hawaii with its 12-month climate. The problem? The competition is already there. In any case, a realistic assessment of the season is crucial.

Surprise!

Yes, now I will recommend going to business school. This book is not about the nuts and bolts of business formation and operation. Business plans, financing, accounting, legal issues, taxation strategies, personnel assessment, income projections, and a host of other issues are the province of a good business school or substitute. You may not need an MBA to run a business, but there is a lot of basic knowledge you had better obtain one way or another. Of course, experience working in a similar business for a period will help. However, much of the financial infrastructure of a business is hidden even from employees.

Good entrepreneurship guides and courses can be invaluable. It is not the job of the bank or start-up venture capital organization to do your business plan for you. Bookkeepers and accountants do not give away their knowledge and experience. Even experienced employees tend to look out for themselves rather than the entire business. You have to learn somewhere and schools are in the business of teaching.

**However, nothing take the place of quality, and
the experience is all you have to sell.**

Now, One More Strategy

Kahneman (2011) introduces a process that he says some say is worth the price of his (or my) book and more. In two pages (pp. 264–265), he introduces the *premortem*.

The technique is simple and may be utilized at any stage of business development. It is System 2 thinking that focuses on the most important issues in developing business strategies. The premortem involves gathering a small group of analysts, preferably more-than-average bright and with some relevant experience. (Does your class qualify?) Their task is to develop a scenario of failure.

Gather a group of knowledgeable people, preferably diverse as to gender, age, and culture. Introduce your business concept and plan including expected markets, management style, and operations focus. Then ask the big question: "Assume that in a year (or two) the business has failed. Write a scenario (story) of how the failure occurred." Time should be limited, perhaps 10 to 20 minutes. Then read the answers aloud and discuss the implications for the plan, including possible remedies for potentially fatal problems.

Does this sound rather negative? Consider how negative you will feel if you develop a business that fulfills the stories. Finally, then, let's look ahead at some stability and change in which a new business will succeed or fail.

Exercise

Do your premortem. If possible, make it a class project. If online, share the project and critiques. Be ruthless (if kind). Remember, this is your life and your money. (It may be play money now, but the real thing someday.)

Questions:
- Are start-up and operating expenses realistic? For how long?
- Are competition estimates realistic?
- What about "black swans," that is, unexpected events?
- What factors produce losses rather than profits?

CHAPTER 15:
LOOKING AHEAD

Is forecasting possible? Kahneman (2011) reports a series of studies on the reliability of predictions of experts and pundits. The overall results are essentially zero. Thus, read anything that follows with a degree of fundamental skepticism. However, there is also the sociological adage that past behavior is the best predictor of future behavior. In the previous 14 chapters, almost all of the analysis has been based on actual behaviors, not speculation of self-appointed "futurists" or otherworldly philosophers. At least, this chapter on looking ahead is largely based on facts.

The Optimistic Bias and "Black Swans"

Not long ago a massive cruise liner lay on its side off the shore of an Italian resort island. Seemingly, the captain steered a course too close to reefs to showboat to those on the island. There were deaths, the loss of a great multidecked cruise liner, and all sorts of fallout. The effects on the Mediterranean cruise business have yet to be calculated. Facts that have come to light such as a design that is so top-heavy that recovery from a few degrees of list may be impossible, lifeboats that cannot be launched from over 15 degrees of tilt, and a crew not trained for disaster management will not do the industry much good. Such an unexpected event is called a "black swan." It is a catastrophic happening that no one anticipates or prepares for. (It is also the case that when warning about such possible events, a person is dismissed as ignorant or biased.)

However, such events can affect the entire structure of an industry. In this case, how many potential cruise clients will picture that great ship lying there as they consider their next trip? Such unexpected associations are always a possibility. Some are enormous such as the effect of Katrina on the Gulf Coast tourism industry. Some are personal such as a bad experience with a rip tide making a beach vacation less attractive.

Another current example: With the gaming industry, did the promoters deliberately ignore the numbers, or were they as naive as the politicians seeking revenue? After all, a casino with its built-in and guaranteed "hold" or house percentage has to be the most reliable profit center in the wide world of leisure businesses. The "nattering nabobs of negativity" who predicted an oncoming saturation of the markets while hundreds of new casinos were opened and proposed were clearly prejudiced. Just ask the developers of Foxwoods in Connecticut who expanded the world's largest casino complex. Oops! Foxwoods teetered on the edge of bankruptcy and could not figure out how to qualify for Chapter 11. Guess what? Even so, neighboring Massachusetts considered legislation to tap their share of the Foxwoods "profits."

Do Not Upset Me With Facts

There is that nasty old WYSIATI (i.e., what you see is all there is) again. When we are sure what will work, that tends to be all we see. Facts such as the number of people within driving distance of a leisure site, the census estimate that 45% of them are poor or near poor, and the general declining trend of participation in the base activity are, if known, overwhelmed by something we think we see.

Case: Change Meets Resistance

Let me give the example of how I could have saved a nameless motorized sports machine company millions (Japanese name withheld to protect me from lawsuit), probably hundreds of millions, if they had taken my advice. They contracted for market advice on motorized winter sports machines. Examining the numbers for markets, I found growth in the rural market related to work and pleasure. My recommendation was that design and products that maximized safety and had a dual use, on the farm and as a family activity, could tap an unrecognized market. This was not what the corporate decision-makers wanted to hear. Committed to an image of speed and power, they went the opposite direction. Then a rash of accidents and lawsuits came along that cost them millions in court costs, damages, and design changes. The point is not that I was so prescient, but that XXXYYY company executives ignored numbers and stayed with their previous commitment.

Probably those reading this will not be in a position to make such a costly error based on WYSIATI and institutional inertia. However, at any level and on any scale, ignoring the numbers and failing to look critically at accepted common wisdom can be costly. What follows is deliberately conservative. Go elsewhere for futurist dreamers who believe that anything that is technologically possible will happen. They have been proven wrong so often that their big book sales and speaking fees ought to be an embarrassment.

Do We Know Anything About the Future?

Absolutely. There will be continuity and change. Most of the change will have central strains of continuity. Most of the continuity will contain elements of change. No trends will be "straight line." Social, economic, and political trends are zigzag, not linear. Even the most confident population forecasts of 20 years ago have proven about half right.

Given that and other RB issues, what are some of the most likely and relevant forecasts? (For a somewhat fuller analysis, see Chapter 12 in *Leisure*, 4th edition [Kelly, 2012].) Here we focus on leisure business implications.

Economic Factors

- Globalization: The travel industry no longer begins at the local agency, but is worldwide and online. Financing is worldwide for once-local developments. Communications and information are online and available to everyone everywhere.

- Employment: Some structural unemployment will outlast recessions with automation replacing manufacturing workers and labor-intensive production chasing low wages. Human services and retailing will employ more women with a majority of mothers in the paid workforce. Skilled R&D (research and development) workers will be rewarded for their long hours and high pressure. For most, predictable "careers" will be supplanted by a series of jobs. Work schedules will be variable with more services operating 24/7.

- Income and wealth: Those with wealth that produces income will continue to do well. Along with costly-to-replace skilled professionals, they will continue to receive disproportionate portions of income, leaving the middle mass as well as the poor and near poor further behind. As a result, high-end markets will receive the most leisure investment attention.

- Value changes: For the affluent, the time–income trade-off may shift somewhat in favor of leisure. However, the market focus on high-end leisure provisions and experiences will continue to have impacts. Will most believe that higher costs produce better experiences? Don't bet against it.

Political Factors

Leisure is unlikely to become a central political issue, at least as long as there is a struggle between those who give primacy to reducing government services and deficits and those who are committed to government services for those with high needs and low resources. However, there are some possible changes in priorities:

- Renewed attention to urban decay and poverty.
- Continued reliance on the market sector for most recreation provisions.
- Tax policies that support particular leisure resources such as the arts. Tax deductions to second homes and big toys used for business will be questioned.
- Comprehensive long-range planning may address issues such as land use and conservation, with resources for recreation included as one factor in the planning. There will continue to be conflicts between planners and some developers, but cooperation in some sites.
- A continued trend toward cost recovery in the administration of public recreation resources and programs.

Demographic Factors

- The graying of America . . . and most of the world. By 2030, over 20% of the U.S. population will be over 65 and the greatest percentage increase will be those over 75 (Ortman, Velkoff, & Hogan, 2014).
- Fertility and family size: Declines in fertility rates slowed after 1990 due to the increase in various ethnic groups. However, delayed marriage for women, rising education levels, labor force participation of women, and early-marriage divorce rates have reduced the number of children desired. Now, the baby boom wave is passing into retirement years.
- Household composition: Increases in female-headed households and a reduction in those headed by married couples to about 50% along with declining marriage rates are changing the old patterns of those seeking "family leisure."

- Diversity: With half or more growth due to immigration, many new citizens will be from Latin America and southern Asia. Ninety percent of the growth has been in the South and Southwest.
- Education levels will increase but with disparities based on income. High cost will continue to challenge programs to make colleges and universities more inclusive.
- The "baby boom" bulge will create RB markets for the retired and then gradually disappear.

Family Factors

- Smaller families, instability, singleness, shorter periods of parenting, and increased female employment are significant factors for leisure. The assumption of the familial household as the primary context of leisure may be changing, with uncertain consequences.
- More recreation may be invested in those who are not part of a couple including single parents.
- Recreation may become a more important context of finding and developing relationships.
- The two-parent assumption for children's recreation programs will be challenged.

Value Orientation Factors

- The diminishing centrality of organized religion seems to open formerly "sacred times" to leisure. Further, recreation often replaces the church as a place of social bonding. Regional differences, however, remain significant.
- The preservation and appreciation of natural environments are emerging as mainstream rather than fringe, even though conflicts continue.
- Will an "experience ethic" for recreation continue to replace the former extrinsic rationales of health and productivity? Maybe.
- Many with some discretion over their work schedules seem to give greater weight to leisure investments without apology. The concept of a balance of work and life now explicitly includes leisure.

A Review of Continuities and Changes

Continuities in Leisure

1. The consistent average 7 to 8% of household income spent on leisure was consistent until about the year 2000. However, there are three recent changes:
   - The 7% average spending on leisure and recreation narrowly defined gradually rose from 1967 to 2007 to about 11%, suggesting the possibility of a value shift or simply more discretionary income. The percentage spent on government declined from 18 to 13% and food and drink from 17.8 to 10.6%. Therefore some of the change may have been due to decreased costs in other areas (Rose, 2012).
   - However, the recession beginning in 2008 reduced spending on leisure, especially for those whose employment is uncertain or interrupted. Recovery spending has increased, but not for everyone. Reduced unemployment should broaden the base for recreation markets. However, the skewed distribution of income would appear to limit lower-50% markets.
   - Other areas of spending have also increased, especially health care from 8 to 18%. So the competition for budget priority continues.

One other trend seems to be that there may be increases in leisure spending among the top 10% in income and decreases among the lowest half or so. In summary, overall continuity may have segments of change within the overall percentages.

2. Overall, the core of leisure will still be accessible activities, especially at home, with outside activities punctuating regular patterns.
3. Despite more irregularities in the life course, primary relationships will remain central to leisure associations and timetables.
4. Time remains scarce for most adults, but will be more variable.
5. The profound changes of the sexual revolution make sexuality and sexual expression recognized as central to leisure meanings and motivations.

6. The stylistic elements of play and display are significant themes of most recreation settings.

7. Distance costs of away-from-home leisure will continue to increase in congested urban areas.

8. Poverty, often intensified by race and ethnicity, produces exclusion from many leisure experiences with alienation evident when the media offer constant images of what the affluent are doing.

9. Shopping continues to be a central activity for most across all demographic lines.

10. Travel remains important even when styles and costs vary widely.

11. Personal leisure investments are an important component of primary relationships for those in committed relationships and those who are not.

12. Developmental goals for those raising children are central recreation investments.

13. Until the year 2000, every younger cohort had a higher education level with resulting diversity of leisure experiences and interests. That trend may become limited by the rising cost of higher education. Also, quantity is not always quality.

14. The quality of relationships remains central to leisure satisfactions.

15. Concerns about the environment may conflict with some recreation uses and developments.

16. The trend toward securing blocks of time such as long weekends will continue, especially when the computer offers the possibility of working from almost anywhere. On the other hand, does the smartphone and laptop degrade recreation experiences?

17. The movement toward more independence and self-reliance of women will make their interests and priorities more central to decisions and plans.

Stop Again

From your experience and observation, which predictions would be most questionable?

Taken one at a time, which changes offer increases in recreation business markets?

How are changes in work schedules likely to affect recreation businesses?

Changes in Leisure

1. The 50-plus age groups will be recognized as major growing markets for all kinds of goods and services. The "active old" are becoming a primary target market for many recreation businesses.
2. Leisure provisions for women will become more diverse and less tied to family.
3. The growing "new class" with discretionary income, education, and control over their schedules will attract disproportionate attention from recreation business developers. They may be the top 20%. What about the middle mass?
4. Off-hour and odd-time leisure will grow with more flexible and irregular work schedules.
5. Sunset activities will usually balance new sunrise recreation, so we need to be alert to change. For example, the shrinking hunting numbers may be balanced by more backpacking.
6. The market sector will come up with more and more recreation implements, programs, toys, and travel offerings, some unrealistic and some on target. Which new ones look promising?
7. More adults will be in periods of transition and/or singleness. Diversity in household composition, and in sexuality, will be more accepted.
8. Business offerings will be more central to recreation provisions and will have greater influence on public decisions about land and infrastructure.
9. Space scarcities will be more acute, in public and private environments.
10. Home and portable electronics will be more diverse and less costly. Many will fit in well with current lifestyles, but will also attract more expenditures through "planned obsolescence."
11. Portability will gain more and more time and attention for communication and entertainment.
12. Mass marketing will increase, but leisure diversity will continue and perhaps increase as well.
13. Focus on high-end clients will saturate many markets, especially as the middle mass commands lower incomes and less purchasing power.
14. Reduced public subsidies in areas such as the arts and outdoor resources will open some markets and close others. Reliance on cost recovery by public providers will make business provisions more competitive for some programs and resources.

15. Threats to retirement income can reduce discretionary income and free time for those in traditional retirement periods of life.
16. New technologies will affect some activities, as fiberglass did to boating and skiing. Not all will be electronic.
17. Nonfamily leisure settings and programs will become more common and more central to business marketing.
18. Health concerns will be important in recreation choices, especially for those aged 50 and above.
19. Travel offerings and packages will become more varied in response to diverse market segments.
20. Many of the more affluent will continue to purchase "big toys" that symbolize their financial status and individualized interests.
21. Conversely, some of the affluent will not want to be tied down to particular locales and schedules so that high-end rentals will flourish.
22. The skills associated with recreation will become more central to choices and meanings as signs of competence in a world where jobs no longer are signs of ability and success.
23. Employed women will be recognized as a market opportunity equal to men. The bias toward male programs and provisions will largely disappear as a mix of gender-segregated, gender-free, and gender-mixed venues will be sought.

In general, an orientation toward variety and diversity for those with discretionary income will be tempered by the financial limits placed on the majority. Diversity will continue to characterize leisure and provide new business opportunities. A heightened awareness of the importance of leisure to human fulfillment and expression could change the budget priorities of some individuals and households.

Stop Again

Every one of the 23 predictions above has implications for changing markets and new opportunities. Either in discussion or a position paper select and analyze those you think most significant for your hopes and plans.

Are the "Small Worlds" Changing?

Yes and no. For the most part, people still live in their immediate environments and with their primary relationships. That means that most leisure is also immediate and with those who are there and convenient. At-home and near-home leisure with household members will continue to dominate time and timetables. Breaking away requires effort and often preplanning.

On the other hand, as repeatedly analyzed, the composition of those small worlds has been changing. Fewer adults and children are in the traditional family with two parents and two children. In fact, having children later in life and sending them on their way has reduced the parenting period from 40 years 100 years ago to about 20 *if* the family stays intact.

There are two implications for recreation businesses. One is the diversity of primary groups that are the basis of a great deal of activity. The second is that at any one time a high proportion of adults are in some period of relationship transition. As discussed, this has implications for marketing and for how a leisure venue is managed and oriented.

Peak Experience, the Real and the Fake

Of course, any recreation business has something to sell. However, a central theme of this book is that the "something" is not really a thing at all. Many business concepts and strategies are focused on what is provided, especially on things that are sold or rented. However, central to the business is the experience, and central to maximizing the experience is what the client is actually doing. Environments are important only as they contribute to the experience. Therefore, it is crucial that we know who the clients are, what they hope for, and what they are really doing.

It is possible that we can argue that the master of "fakery," the Disney organization, seems to produce a lot of positive experiences wherein nothing is authentic. One reason probably is that their visitors come expecting the best in quality and get it. Quality works almost every time. On the other hand, most leisure businesses are designed to attract and keep clients who want to repeat good, and sometimes great, experiences. This means that entertainment is not enough. Recreation clients act and interact in ways that meet their sense of self, expression, ability, and development. (See Chapters 13 and 14.)

The Question No One Can Answer for You

In the end, all of the analysis and possibilities of a recreation business investment and strategy bring the potential entrepreneur back to a more fundamental question that one no one else can answer: What do you want your life to be like?

If you want security and guarantees, then probably a recreation-based business is not for you. If you want a somewhat open-ended future, involvement with people who are often at their best, the excitement of being able to try out novel possibilities, a sense that what you are doing is uniquely your own, and the risk of living and working in an open environment, then an RB may be what you are seeking. No one said life would be easy. But the challenge that is met with skill can be central to creating and operating a business as well as to being a satisfied RB client. No formulas, but lots of possibilities.

Remember, you will be planning for your own peak experiences as well as others'.

REFERENCES

Bureau of Labor Statistics. (n.d.). Employment by major industry sector, 2006, 2016, and projected 2026 [Table]. Retrieved January 10, 2017, from https://www.bls.gov/emp/ep_table_201.htm

Csikszentmihalyi, M. (1976). *Beyond boredom and anxiety*. San Francisco, CA: Jossey-Bass.

Galbraith, J. K. (1958). *The affluent society*. Boston, MA: Houghton-Mifflin.

Kelly, J. R. (2012). *Leisure* (4th ed.). Urbana, IL: Sagamore.

Kelly, J. R. (1987). *Peoria winter*. Lexington, MS: D.C. Heath.

Kelly, J. R., & Warnick, R. (1999). *Recreation trends and markets: The 21st century*. Urbana, IL: Sagamore.

Kahneman, D. (2011). *Thinking fast and slow*. New York, NY: Farrar, Straus, and Giroux.

Ortman, J. M., Velkoff, V. A., & Hogan, H. (2014, May). *Population Estimates and Projections. An aging nation: The older population in the United States* (P25-1140). Retrieved from https://www.census.gov/prod/2014pubs/p25-1140.pdf

Pine, J., & Gilmore, J. (1999). *The experience economy*. Boston, MA: Harvard Business School Press.

Raymond, L. C. P. (1985). *The effects of unemployment on the leisure behavior of unemployed steelworkers (expenditure, activity, satisfaction, family, Chicago, Illinois)* (Doctoral disseration). Retrieved from https://www.ideals.illinois.edu/handle/2142/70942

Reeves, R. (2017). *Dream hoarders*. Washington, DC: Brookings Institution.

Rose, S. J. (2012, April). How we spend. *The Atlantic*. Retrieved from https://www.theatlantic.com/magazine/archive/2012/04/how-we-spend/308906/

Rubin, J. (Ed.). (2016). *Theme index and museum index: The global attractions attendance report*. Retrieved from Themed Entertainment Association website: http://www.teaconnect.org/images/files/TEA_235_1 03719_170601.pdf

Stebbins, R. (1979). *Amateurs: On the Margin between work and leisure*. Beverly Hills, CA: Sage.

U.S. Census Bureau. (n.d.). Statistical Abstracts series. Retrieved from https://www.census.gov/library/publications/time-series/statistical_abstracts.html

Veblen, T. (1953). *The theory of the leisure class*. New York, NY: New American Library. (Original work published 1899)

APPENDIX:
TEACHING METHODS

To begin, the entire learning premise of this book is that students learn best by engaging in discussion, debate, critical analysis of every-thing (including the text), and doing their own research, if on a small scale. Conversely, they learn least well, if at all, listening to 50-minute lectures or plowing through long chapters of a text the night before an exam.

Therefore, the text is continually interrupted with questions, debate topics, and mini–research projects. Obviously, many or most will not be relevant in any specific course setting. Many or most will not interest the class. Some may be assigned as homework, some assigned for extra credit, and some ignored. That's ok. Be flexible.

Also, many will need to be adapted for an online course. I am a be-liever in writing, but not what is common in education. Rather than write everything one can think of, sometimes relevant and sometimes not, the writer needs to be concise. What is left out may be as impor-tant to quality as what is stressed. One method is the one-page paper in which the instructor refuses to read beyond the bottom of the first page. (After all, this is good practice for doing a business plan, a corporate memo, or instructions to a business staff.) Good writing and editing are useful in any setting.

What about exams? If they cannot be avoided, then again I recom-mend formats such as (1) outlining one side of a debate in a page or less (and presuming that there is no right or wrong position, only weak or unsubstantiated arguments). (2) Again in a page, take on any of the questions or issues in the boxes in the text. (3) Prepare an argument for class discussion. Or (4) redo an issue from the developing business plan. All this assumes that the major project, the Business Plan, will be a big chunk of the final grade.

I realize that this threatens the instructor-as-final-authority model of teaching and stresses the experience of the students. Class learning ought to be a communal enterprise, not sheer competition for grades. (Yes, this calls for the end of grading on the curve. I sometimes began a class by stating that everyone begins with an *A*, but maintaining it may call for some real work.) Students who want a credit, not a learning ex-perience, should try another class.

ABOUT THE AUTHOR

John R. (Jack) Kelly is Professor Emeritus at the University of Illinois at Urbana-Champaign. He was Professor in Leisure Studies and the Institute for Human Development and Director of the Gerontology and Aging Studies program. His PhD in sociology is from the University of Oregon, and he received master's degrees from Yale, Southern California, and Oregon.

He is the author of 12 books including four editions of *Leisure*, *Leisure Business Strategies*, and *Recreation Business*, the first text in that field. *Freedom to Be: A New Sociology of Leisure* is a graduate-level analysis. He is editor of *Activity and Aging* and coauthor of *Recreation Trends and Markets in the 21st Century* and *21st Century Leisure: Current Issues*. His books have been translated and published in China and Japan. He has authored over 100 research articles, chapters, encyclopedia articles, and technical reports. He has had consulting contracts with American and Japanese corporations including General Motors, Battelle International, and Yamaha as well as the U.S. Forest Service, U.S. Park Service, and State of Illinois.

Among honors he has received are the Roosevelt Research Award, the National Literary Award, and Distinguished Colleague Award from the National Recreation and Park Association. At the University of Illinois, he received two awards for research excellence and was Nash Scholar of the American Association of Leisure and Recreation. He was founding Chair of the Research Commission of World Leisure and has lectured and taught worldwide.

Among his own recreation engagements have been 54 years as a pilot; 40 years of tennis; choral singing; a little cowboying in Montana; basic training of horses; and reading in fields such as economics, politics, and history. He was a college baseball pitcher and played three sports in high school. He is the proud father of two daughters, Professor Susan Kelly of the University of Exeter and Professor Janice Kelly of Purdue University, and has two fine grandsons. He and his wife, Ruth Kelly, live in retirement on Jekyll Island, Georgia, and Beaver Island, Michigan.

INDEX

Stebbins, Robert, 69, 70, 108
student projects, 49–51

T

target markets
    advertising, 91
    assessing, 71–72
    bias, 74–75
    big markets, 66–67
    missing the target, 68–69
    national or global markets, 123–124
    niche markets and leisure subcultures, 69–70
    numbers not everything, 72–73
    probabilities and personal judgment, 65
    promise of associations, relationships, 74
    trend or fad?, 61–64
taxation, 57
teaching methods, 171
Telemark, 32
television retailers, 66
theater
    business as, 114–115
    metaphor for leisure experience, 135
Thinking Fast and Slow (Kahneman), 42
time
    blockage for participation, 130–131
    as scarce resource and leisure as choice, 77–78
    "seize the day," 84–85
    timetables and schedules, 85–86
tourism, literary, 73
trade organizations, 7

traumatic events and life course, 99
travel agencies, 58
trend analysis, 150
trends or fads, 61–64

U

undercapitalization, 53, 117
U.S. Forest Service, 83

V

Veblen, Thorstein, 28, 29
video game parlors, 63

W

Walmart, 59
Walt Disney World, 104
Walt Disney Worlds, 121–122
weather, 80–81
weather.com, 80
wild river rafting businesses, 48
women
    employment of, 85
    increases in female-headed households, 160
    playing golf, 0
work bias, 74–75
WYSIATI (what you see is all there is), 43–44, 47, 158

Y

Yamaha, 119
youth sports, 104

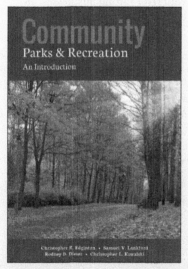